THE MODERN PROPER

Simple Dinners for Every Day

Holly Erickson and Natalie Mortimer

Photography by Eva Kolenko

SIMON ELEMENT   New York London Toronto Sydney New Delhi

SIMON
ELEMENT

1230 Avenue of the Americas
New York, NY 10020

First Simon Element hardcover edition April 2022

SIMON ELEMENT and colophon are registered trademarks of
Simon & Schuster, Inc.

For information about special discounts for bulk purchases, please
contact Simon & Schuster Special Sales at 1-866-506-1949 or
business@simonandschuster.com.

The Simon & Schuster Speakers Bureau can bring authors to your
live event. For more information or to book an event, contact the
Simon & Schuster Speakers Bureau at 1-866-248-3049 or visit
our website at www.simonspeakers.com.

Interior design by Laura Palese

Manufactured in China

10 9 8 7 6 5 4 3 2 1

Library of Congress Cataloging-in-Publication Data is available.

ISBN 978-1-9821-7766-9
ISBN 978-1-9821-7767-6 (ebook)

FOR ANDERS,
ELSA, JONES,
RAMONA,
SCOUT, AND
WALLACE

Contents

ALL DAY EGGS

MEATLESS

CHICKEN

PORK AND BEEF

SEAFOOD

MEATBALLS

SOUP

THINGS FOR DIPPING, SPREADING, AND DRESSING

Thanks for picking up our book.

Before we were two work-from-home mom-on-the-go veterans with babies on our hips and recipe experiments in our fridge, we were young girls with a passion for the culinary.

For Natalie, that meant hours watching her grandma pack the perfect pierogi or simmer her meat sauce until it was "just so."

"This is the proper way to dice," she'd say as her wrinkled hand guided the knife down the crisscrossed cuts of an onion. Everything was the "proper" this and the "proper" that, leaving little room for mistakes or new ideas.

Growing up, Natalie's mom always put a hot dinner on the table, but that dinner typically consisted of steamed vegetables and a plain baked chicken breast. Healthy, warm, and balanced, but often just that. It wasn't until a nannying job in high school that Natalie's eyes opened to the many flavors and ingredients she hadn't yet discovered. One night her employer rushed out and left her with a whole chicken and a long list of instructions. This scene might have overwhelmed your average teenager, but not Natalie. She began preparing a honey mustard marinade, roasted the chicken, and shredded it into a salad with goat cheese, pistachios, and diced mangos. She was immediately hooked and looked forward to work, where she'd raid this family's kitchen for exciting produce, grains, and cuts of meat she'd never even heard of. After her first encounter with such an array of whole foods, there was no turning back.

On one weekend mall trip with her friends, after a visit to the Cafe Nordstrom and the first slurp of their famous tomato basil soup, Natalie spent her hard-earned nannying income on her first cookbook, the store's. From there, she unlocked dishes like a pear, walnut, and gorgonzola salad and shrimp simmered in spicy cream sauce.

Holly, too, turned outside of her family's kitchen to fulfill her craving for cooking. In fourth grade, she signed up for her first cooking class, offered by her community. Much like Natalie had been with her grandma, in class Holly also was exposed to the correct techniques. There seemed to be a "right" way and a "wrong" way to accomplish each task and make every dish.

You might say Holly's journey from community-class lasagna to gourmet everything began out of jealousy . . . well, sort of. After dinner at a friend's home where every dish was cooked directly out of the latest issue of *Bon Appétit*, Holly's new husband couldn't stop raving about the food. Before marrying, Scott had rarely eaten vegetables at home that didn't come from a can. He acted like his life had been changed, and Holly immediately subscribed to the magazine.

Holly soon found herself wowing friends, too. She'd add pesto to homemade tomato soup (also her favorite) and serve grilled cheese on good sourdough bread with quality cheddar. Today, it seems so simple, but at the time, her friends were used to cold deli sandwiches and potato chips at gatherings. Soon, they were raving like Scott had been. She sat back and watched how the hot soup and perfectly crusty sandwich made everyone feel. The effect a homemade meal had on those around her was intoxicating. She had to create more, cook more, host more! The occasional gathering of friends turned into dinner clubs, which turned into a catering gig, and . . .

Fast-forward to the early 2000s, when jeans were low-rise and our still kid-free lives were flexible enough to allow our husbands to take off together on a carefree, eight-week-long band tour. (Yes—that's how we met! Holly's new husband was live-painting the shows while Natalie's husband-to-be kept rhythm on the drums.) In 2009, Holly and Scott found themselves migrating from their Pacific Northwest roots to make a home in Texas. As the years went by, a long-distance friendship formed. Whenever we were together, our husbands bonded over art, music, and the like, while we found ourselves nerding out about the menus for the next big baby shower we were throwing, or for the friend's backyard birthday soiree we were helping plan. Food always dominated our conversations.

In 2012, Holly and her family moved back up to the PNW, landing in the same city as Natalie and Mort. Babies were born. New homes were purchased. Our husbands began working together at the same creative agency. There was much to talk about! But food . . .

Food was always top of mind and tip of tongue.

It was during one of our many initial food-focused conversations that we realized we'd had similar food obsessions in our young adulthoods. We also discovered our shared hobby of folding up paper menus from restaurants and bringing them home to study later. Each time our friends took us to new local spots, we'd snag these like an elderly woman hoards sugar packets. Holly even went so far as to file all of her collected menus, so she could easily dissect the ingredients and experiment with food in her home kitchen later.

Aside from the grooming from Natalie's overly opinionated grandmother and Holly's lackluster time in a church basement, we were both self-taught cooks. These early influences trailed us into our kitchens in the years following as we ventured out and fell in love—with hosting and feeding of our nearest and dearest. But clearly, we had both left these humble beginnings to slowly shed the weight of the rigid rules we'd been taught, refining our palates along the way. Separately, we carved our paths to hospitality. We had each created a blog, venturing into the daunting world of recipe creation on our own. We were learning to write our own food stories and capture and edit photos, all while nursing babies and trying to budget groceries for our families. It was not for the faint of heart. And doing it alone felt impossible.

In August 2013, we took our kids out on an oh-so-PNW berry-picking adventure. As usual, we began to gush over all we could do with the ingredients.

"These would make a killer cobbler."

"No, a galette!"

"Oh, or an arugula salad!"

Our hike ended with a bounty of berries—and the resolve to join forces and start our own brand together.

We set out to reinvent the idea of "proper" and the lost art of hospitality for the modern homemaker. Our original intent was to capture hosting in all its forms, and to make enough money to afford higher-quality food for our families. If we could up our grocery budgets, stock our pantries like the family Natalie had nannied for, and wow our friends more often, we'd be content. Not exactly pie-in-the-sky dreams, but definitely a worthy pursuit! In our early planning meetings, we'd sip coffee in each other's living rooms while simultaneously kissing our kids' owies and calming their tantrums.

And so The Modern Proper was born.

The Early Days

We built a calendar for that first year, and we planned. We would focus on all the major holidays and feature not only food, but also decor and Do It Yourself crafts.

First up? Valentine's Day. We decorated Holly's entire house—it looked like Saint Valentine had thrown up on the place. We were spray-painting, die-cutting, and lost in a sea of crafts. Yes, there were pancakes, but we had very much lost track of why we had started this whole thing. When Natalie's oldest son awoke that morning with a 103-degree fever and she still dressed him in red and made him smile for a photo, we knew we weren't exactly living the blogger life we had envisioned.

Our kids got older. Our lives got busier. Crafting and DIY no longer made sense for us. We shifted gears to what actually worked for us, and as a result, our recipes naturally became more streamlined and approachable. We decided to create meals that were adventurous, but never intimidating. We wanted food lovers with full lives and limited time (like us) to know a boring dinner was never the only option. Above all, we wanted each meal to remind people of the simple joy of pausing to gather around the table.

Thanks to social media, we immediately heard how much our recipes were saving people's weeknight routines. The type of feedback that had warmed Holly's heart at her first dinner party was now right in the palm of our hands. That also meant we knew right away when something didn't work. "I would make this if it didn't have 25 ingredients!" read one of our early comments. After our fragile egos recovered, we yet again reinvented "proper" and simplified even further. After all, we wanted people to actually cook our recipes!

In 2016, we were nominated for the *Saveur* Blog Awards in the Most Inspired Weeknight Dinners category. While clinking glasses in New York City and feeling pretty good about ourselves, we realized that Inspired Weeknight Dinners really were our greatest challenge and our greatest joy. We were weeknight dinner girls through and through—we were not hot-glue-gun fanatics, and we were definitely not bakers. We realized dinner is a problem everyone has to solve every day. And as the demands of our increasingly busy schedules kept us from more elaborate cooking feats, we learned to be smarter about what we made and how we made it.

So maybe we don't have forty-five minutes to whip up tomato sauce from scratch on a Wednesday night. But we can take what we love about that sauce and make it work for us. Simmer a little butter into a jar of store-bought marinara and, hello there, ten-minute dinner! This is cooking The Modern Proper way. Like our readers, we are always looking for efficiency at every turn, but without sacrificing flavor.

So, What's for Dinner?

Every recipe in this book serves as a simple solution to that perennial problem. Whether you're a novice or a pro, a busy parent or a workaholic, our goal is to arm you in the kitchen with what you need to make cooking work for you. If you're the type who finds themselves ripping out recipes from glossy culinary magazines, but never seems to get around to making that fancy meal, you've come to the right place. The longing to live and eat gourmet, whole, delicious foods is real—and the struggle to get there holds back many closeted foodies. We don't want your sweat-suit uniform, untidied house, or basic spice cabinet to keep you from good food. Forget the "fancy" and focus on the food—the food that will gather friends and family.

We've spent years filling our toolbox with basic culinary tricks. Want food that tastes like it's been cooked over an open flame without having to actually do it at the end of a long week? Add smoked paprika to, well, pretty much anything. And there's plenty more where that came from, like drying chicken with a paper towel to ensure extra-crispy skin, using a fork to remove the leaves from the stalks of herbs, or partially freezing your meat before cutting it for extra-thin slices. We're ready to equip you, fellow food lover.

From the Clean-Out-the-Pantry Pasta (page 84) to the Sweet and Sticky Pork and Asparagus (page 156), all the recipes here are doable. No ingredient is too difficult to find—if it's not at your grocery store, it's just a few clicks away. You should always feel like you can work with what's at your fingertips and in your freezer, so we've offered plenty of options and swaps throughout the book.

And you'll find one-pot meals because none of us gets into cooking for the dirty dishes (no matter how rockin' your sudsy playlist might be). Because at the end of the day our first love is hosting, many recipes are meant to feed a family or a table of friends.

This Book

We organized the book pretty traditionally, separating it mostly by the main ingredients we know you like to cook with. The first of those is eggs, which we strongly believe are meant for way more than just breakfast. After meatless dishes and the usual proteins, you'll find meatballs, a most beloved staple we believe can hold any flavor profile in a single bite. More meatballs, please! We separated out soups because we thought you might want them on repeat during the colder months, like we do. And finally, you'll find recipes for our go-to sauces and condiments. Why buy when you can make your own—and make them better?

We've also added some quick-reference tags for when you're recipe hunting for something very specific. With the flip of a page and a fast glance, you'll be able to spot recipes that fall into the following categories: <35 Minutes, Dairy-Free, Gluten-Free, Kid-Friendly, Sheet Pan, and/or Vegetarian. Sure, we could have kept going, but we know you well enough to know these features go hand in hand with figuring out what's for dinner on any given night.

This book is meant to expand your "go-to" list and to help you explore new territory. Our goal is for every home cook to graduate to a place where cooking can be intuitive and creative. Never allow someone else's definition of "proper" keep you from creating elevated meals your way.

Ingredients

A reader—let's call her Jane—once sent us a message saying she hadn't had any red wine vinegar on hand for a recipe, so she'd combined distilled white vinegar with her leftover merlot and was surprised when the recipe didn't taste quite right. While we definitely don't recommend that, we will call out as many ingredient swaps as we can, both here and throughout the book, so these recipes can work for you as often and as easily as possible. And when you really can't make a sub, we'll make sure you know it so you don't end up like Jane.

This list is not a comprehensive counting of every last thing in our pantries. We work with food day in and day out, so our kitchens are a bit more stocked than most. Rather, these are the star ingredients that have swept in and rescued us time after time and that will, therefore, appear over and over again in the recipes ahead. They're all familiar and findable—after all, the last thing we'd want to do is to send you on a wild goose chase after something obscure that'll go largely unused in the back of your cupboard. Having these key ingredients on hand will set you up for success in making most, if not all, of the recipes in this book.

EGGS

Eggs stay good for weeks in the fridge, so they're pretty easy to keep around. Especially for a recipe in which the egg is front and center, you'll want to use the best large eggs you can buy. In the grocery store, look for the words "pastured" and "free-range" on the label. Or better yet, head to the farmers' market for fresh, local eggs of the highest quality and flavor. If you have any questions, a quick conversation with the vendor will tell you everything you need to know.

BUTTER

Throughout this book, we use both salted and unsalted butter, and each serves its own purpose. We like salted for things like sautéing shrimp or spreading on good bread, and unsalted for baking or in recipes that have a lot of other salty ingredients. If you're going to keep just one kind on hand, make it unsalted. It's more versatile, since it can be used in sweet or savory dishes, and you can always add salt if needed.

SALT

Salt is easily our desert-island ingredient. We're crazy for it, and in awe of its incredible transformative power. In a perfect world, you'd keep three sizes of salt crystals in the pantry at all times: flaky, kosher, and fine. Flaky salt is the largest crystal, and we use it for finishing dishes. Kosher salt is coarse, but smaller than flaky salt, and we use it the most since it's so versatile (think a big pinch of salt added to pasta water, or a sprinkle over vegetables before grilling). The last is fine salt, which we mostly use in dressings and sauces, where it dissolves nicely. All three sizes are produced not only from rock salt (such as Himalayan), which is mined, but also from sea salt, which is evaporated from seawater; and salts from different origins have differences in mineral content, flavor, and saltiness. Taste a variety and choose the ones you like best. If you're going to pick just one for cooking, however, make it kosher salt: It can stand in for the other two in a pinch.

OIL

We draw a lot of our culinary inspiration from the cultures that ring the Mediterranean, so it's no surprise that extra-virgin olive oil is one of the most ubiquitous ingredients in this book. Extra-virgin olive oil is, quite simply, the best of the best. Depending

on the olive varieties used and the region it comes from, the taste of this incredibly healthy, richly golden oil will vary vastly from bottle to bottle. Have fun exploring! It can be pricey, so we use it in recipes where the buttery, peppery, fruity flavors will really shine, to make ultra-delicious vinaigrettes, or to finish off a dish. For cooking that involves high heat, we reach for neutral oil with a higher smoke point (meaning it won't start smoking until it gets very, very hot). For this type of cooking, we call for vegetable oil throughout the book, but feel free to use any neutral oil you prefer—avocado, canola, corn, grapeseed, or peanut oil will work just fine.

VINEGAR

Vinegar can be tricky. While we want to say you can get away with only stocking one kind, that's just not true. To make the recipes in this book, you'll need a few. The good news is that all of these vinegars are widely available and inexpensive, so it's not a big deal to stock up. And having the right kind for the right recipe makes all the difference. We recommend keeping rice vinegar, unfiltered apple cider vinegar, distilled white vinegar, red wine vinegar, and balsamic vinegar in your pantry.

STOCK

Soups are big in our world, and there's no soup without stock, so we always have a lot of it on hand. And we do mean stock—we prefer it to broth. Stock is always made with animal bones, so it is richer and more nutritious than broth, which doesn't necessarily include bones and is generally not cooked for as long. That said, they're relatively interchangeable, so feel free to use broth if that's what you have. We like the low-sodium kind, so we can control the saltiness in the recipe ourselves. Tetra Paks are quick and convenient, but cans are fine, too. If you're short on space, grab yourself some Better Than Bouillon. The little jars of stock concentrate are terrific space-savers and last a long time in the fridge. If you go with bouillon, start with just a little bit. You can always add more, but there's no going back once you've added too much.

SPICES

There are a handful of spices you'll reach for over and over again as you cook your way through this book and (hopefully) make a few of our go-to DIY spice blends. Buy the best quality you can, and always make sure your spices are fresh. Different spices have different shelf lives—for example, whole spices last longer than pre-ground—so be sure yours are well within their good-by date.

- Black peppercorns
- Chili powder
- Cumin
- Granulated garlic
- Onion powder
- Paprika (sometimes this will be labeled sweet paprika or Hungarian paprika)
- Smoked paprika
- Yellow curry powder

CHILI PASTE

We like spicy food, so our pantries bear a vague resemblance to the hot sauce aisle at the grocery store, and at least one (and usually more) jar of Asian chili paste is always in the mix. Sambal oelek, an Indonesian chili paste, is our go-to because it is so simple—

just chilies, vinegar, and salt. It goes well with many dishes and doesn't compete much with other flavors. Garlic-chili paste and sriracha also have a place in our hearts, and if you prefer them to sambal, feel free to stock them instead. Or make like us and load up on all three.

BREADCRUMBS

Breadcrumbs are a go-to for us, and you'll see us use them over and over again in the recipes ahead. In meatballs, they act as an indispensable binding agent, but we also think of them as a handy way to add a crunch to the top of just about any pasta or salad. Panko—a type of Japanese breadcrumb—is by far our favorite, and it's easy to find. Light, airy, and flaky in texture, panko is made from bread flakes rather than breadcrumbs, and so it brings the unique crispy-crunchiness we crave.

SOY SAUCE

No kitchen is complete without soy sauce or tamari. Made from fermented soybeans, it flavors our favorite stir-fries, dressings, and sauces. We always prefer low-sodium soy sauce because it gives us more control over the finished flavor of whatever we're making. Tamari is soy sauce's (usually) gluten-free twin. It is traditionally made without wheat, and most brands are fully gluten-free, but always check the label to be sure. You can make a 1:1 swap for soy sauce. If you're looking for a soy-free alternative to both soy sauce and tamari, coconut aminos are a near-perfect sub. We also happen to love the way they taste. They have about a quarter of the sodium and a lovely, light sweetness. We'd suggest you stock both soy sauce (or tamari) and coconut aminos, but if you don't have coconut aminos, it's not a big deal (see Note on page 156).

RED CURRY PASTE

Our love for red curry paste grew naturally out of our love for Thai food. It's one of our very favorite bang-for-buck ingredients. One little container packs so much punch. Loaded with chilies, lemongrass, galangal, lime leaves, and (usually) shrimp paste or fish sauce, curry paste is densely flavorful and surprisingly versatile. Ingredients vary from brand to brand, so do a little taste-testing and see which you prefer. We're especially loyal to Mae Ploy and generally prefer brands that include shrimp paste, but you can find versions without it if you have an allergy or are looking for a vegan option.

HERBS

If you're not in the habit of cooking with fresh herbs, get ready to up your game. Whenever you see us call for fresh basil, chives, cilantro, or parsley, please really use fresh! That said, for many other herbs, you can swap dried without sacrificing much in flavor. Just be sure to halve the amount called for in the recipe if you make the swap, as dried herbs pack a lot more punch. As a general rule, avoid using dried herbs as a finish or garnish because they will be, well, dry.

BRINY SALTY BITS

Capers, olives, anchovies—these little jars of salt-brined, umami-giving goodness are pantry superheroes. They take up virtually no space at all, they last for ages, and they can bring a whole meal to life.

SHALLOTS AND ONIONS

We call for both of these sharp, fragrant alliums frequently in this book, and while we recommend you use what we call for, they can be interchanged in a pinch. Shallots have a unique sweetness and delicacy that sets them apart from regular yellow onions. The good news is that if you store them in a dark, cool place, both shallots and onions keep well for months, so it's pretty easy to have both on hand, even if you're not going through them quickly.

PARMESAN

Ah, Parmigiano-Reggiano, aka Parmesan—the one and only. Accept no substitutes and definitely don't bother with the pre-grated stuff. Just don't. Aside from being less flavorful, it usually has an anti-caking additive that keeps it from melting the way you want it to. This salty Italian cow's-milk cheese is one of a kind, and yes, it's expensive. But a little bit of the real stuff goes a long way. We use a Microplane to grate it over pasta; if you want it to be superfine, remove the rind, plop a hunk in a high-speed blender, and watch it turn to the cheese dust that dreams are made of.

Equipment

If your kitchen isn't well equipped or if you're just getting started, it will be useful to know some of the tools we've found to be absolutely essential. As with almost anything you do around the house, having the right tool for the job is half the battle. Some are very budget-friendly, and a few are a bit of a splurge, but all will make your days in the kitchen go just a bit more smoothly.

NONSTICK SKILLET

We suggest investing in a set of nonstick skillets that includes two or three sizes. We use them multiple times a day, for everything from scrambled eggs to meatballs, and having a few sizes to choose from is handy. Take care not to scratch them with metal utensils; use only wooden or silicone and the skillets will last and last.

CAST-IRON SKILLET

One big cast-iron skillet will take you far—look for one that's at least twelve inches in diameter. For searing a perfect steak or roasting a chicken, cast iron can't be beat.

DUTCH OVEN AND/OR BRAISER

We love these gorgeous kitchen workhorses so much that we really do think it's worth making space in your kitchen for both, if you're able. That said, if you're only going to buy one, start with a Dutch oven and put a braiser on your wish list for the future. Because it's deeper, a Dutch oven is slightly more versatile. Available in a wide range of vibrant colors, these lidded pots go seamlessly from stovetop to oven to tabletop, making for effortlessly beautiful meals.

SHEET PAN

You might be today years old when you realize you *really* need a sheet pan—we can't live without ours. If you're shopping online, it can feel like you need a bakers' dictionary to determine the difference between the full, half, and quarter sizes. We almost always go with a rimmed half-sheet pan. It prevents everything from spilling off the sides, and it fits perfectly in our ovens.

KNIVES

Good knives are nonnegotiable, and you'll need a few. Get yourself a bread knife, paring knife, eight- or nine-inch chef's knife, and a pair of kitchen shears that can be sharpened. Even the fanciest, most expensive knives will dull after months of daily use, so an electric knife-sharpener is a smart investment, too. (If that's one thing too many, most kitchen stores can do it for you.)

FOOD PROCESSOR

For making pesto, hummus, and any number of sauces, spreads, and dips, a food processor makes life so much easier. We find a mini useful to have around, but if you're going to get one, a seven-cup should do everything you need it to.

IMMERSION BLENDER

These handheld wonders are worth their weight in truffles, and are ideal for when you want to blend a sauce or soup right in the pot. If you're using a regular blender instead, just be sure to let the liquid cool slightly before you transfer it from the pot.

MICROPLANE GRATER

You'll find a myriad of uses for a Microplane once it's sitting in your utensil drawer. It's ideal for Parmesan and citrus zest, but it's also terrific for grating fresh garlic or ginger—it almost liquefies them, so they meld easily into whatever dish you're adding them to.

MANUAL CITRUS JUICER

Sure, you can juice a lemon by wiggling a fork into the pulp, but the seeds usually get into the juice you do manage to squeeze out, and, well, it's just not a great user experience. Enter the manual citrus juicer! It's easily the greatest life upgrade you can make for less than twenty dollars.

PEPPER GRINDER

Freshly cracked pepper is essential, and so you'll need a pepper grinder. You'll probably use it multiple times a day, so go ahead and get yourself a nice one! We like the kinds that have multiple grind settings—larger pieces for topping off soup or pasta, finer pieces for mixing in.

INSTANT-READ THERMOMETER

This tool really is essential, both for making sure your meat is not overdone and for food safety. Here's a handy guide to doneness temperatures for some of the most commonly used cuts of meat:

Pork	Poultry	Beef
Medium: 145°F	165°F	Rare: 125°F
Well: 160°F		Medium-rare: 135°F
		Medium: 145°F
		Medium-well: 150°F
		Well: 160°F

SHALLOW BOWLS

Keep three or four shallow bowls around, as they'll come in handy for dredging. Old pie pans also work wonderfully for this task; they're cheap and don't need to be fancy at all, but we've found that they're the perfect size and depth.

ALL DAY EGGS

Serves 6
Prep Time: 5 Minutes
Cook Time: 6 Minutes 30 Seconds
<35 Minutes
Dairy-Free
Gluten-Free
Kid-Friendly
Vegetarian

6 large eggs

SOFT-BOILED EGGS

A perfect, sunny, runny soft-boiled egg makes the ideal finishing crown for so many of our favorite almost-meals. A pot of lentils becomes lunch (or a light dinner) when topped with an egg. Same goes for most salads. A few slices of fresh, peak-summer tomato piled on good bread becomes a real feast when finished with one of these jammy beauts. And guess what? Making an egg that looks this terrific is completely achievable, even if you've never boiled an egg before. We've got the whole process down to a paint-by-numbers level of foolproof. You've got this!

1. Place a folded kitchen towel in the bottom of a large pot. Fill the pot two thirds of the way with water, place over high heat, and bring to a boil. Once your water starts to boil, use a slotted spoon to lower the eggs, one at a time, into the water. Cook the eggs for 6 minutes 30 seconds.

2. While the eggs are boiling, fill a medium bowl with ice water.

3. As soon as the timer goes off, using a slotted spoon, transfer the eggs to the ice bath. Let sit for 5 minutes to stop the cooking. Drain.

4. Carefully tap around the rounded bottom end of the egg to crack it open. Peel and use the eggs as desired. Store refrigerated in an airtight container for up to 2 days.

CARAMELIZED ONION FRITTATA WITH BACON AND CHIVES

Serves 6
Prep Time: 10 Minutes
Cook Time: 20 Minutes
<35 Minutes
Gluten-Free

We think of the frittata as the Italian spinoff of a classic French omelette, with room to add mix-ins and make delicious flavor combinations. In fact, a frittata is a lot like a quiche in that way—a savory egg pie—but without the crust. This particular version is a favorite of ours; the caramelized onions lend a rich, earthy sweetness, and, well, bacon is never a bad decision. A pour of heavy cream gives the eggs a gorgeous texture, so don't skip it! Pair it with roasted potatoes or a simple green salad alongside at breakfast, dinner, or any meal in between. And one last thing to mention: It's every bit as good cold as it is warm.

1. Preheat the oven to 400°F with a rack in the center position.

2. In a large bowl, beat the eggs. Add the cream, ¾ cup of the cheese, the chives, fine salt, and pepper. Stir to combine.

3. Heat the olive oil in a 10-inch, ovenproof skillet over medium heat. Once the oil is glistening, add half of the kale and cook, stirring, until slightly wilted, about 1 minute. Add the remaining kale and continue cooking, stirring, until completely wilted, about 3 more minutes. Stir in the caramelized onions and crumbled bacon to incorporate.

4. Pour the egg mixture over the kale mixture and give it a quick stir to incorporate the eggs and filling evenly. Cook, undisturbed, until the edges are set, about 2 minutes. Transfer the skillet to the oven and bake until the eggs are completely set, about 10 minutes. The eggs shouldn't move when you jiggle the pan.

5. Top the frittata with the remaining ¼ cup cheese and the extra chives. Slice into wedges. Sprinkle with flaky salt to taste, and then serve.

8 large eggs

⅓ cup heavy cream

4 ounces feta or goat cheese, crumbled (about 1 cup)

¼ cup chopped fresh chives, plus more for serving

1 teaspoon fine sea salt

½ teaspoon freshly cracked black pepper

2 tablespoons extra-virgin olive oil

4 cups kale, tough stems discarded and leaves roughly chopped

1 cup Caramelized Onions (page 265)

6 to 8 slices cooked bacon, crumbled

Flaky salt, for serving

Makes 6 tacos
Prep Time: 10 minutes
Cook Time: 10 minutes
<35 Minutes
Gluten-Free
Kid-Friendly
Vegetarian

CHIPOTLE SAUCE

½ cup mayonnaise

2 teaspoons fresh lime juice
(from 1 lime)

2 teaspoons chopped chipotle
peppers in adobo plus
1 tablespoon adobo sauce

TACOS

6 large eggs

½ teaspoon fine sea salt

2 tablespoons vegetable oil or
extra-virgin olive oil

6 (6-inch) flour tortillas

1 cup roughly broken tortilla chips

½ cup pico de gallo

½ cup shredded pepper Jack
cheese

¼ cup loosely packed fresh
cilantro leaves

1 avocado, pitted and sliced

MIGAS BREAKFAST TACOS

Since Holly moved to Austin in 2020, Natalie's "work visits" to the Lone Star State always end up being more about finding the best hole-in-the-wall eateries . . . which is research, right? If you know anything about Austin's food scene, you know that breakfast tacos are its beating heart. After trying out approximately twelve thousand variations, we agreed our very favorites were those filled with migas, a classic Tex-Mex breakfast of eggs scrambled with crispy tortillas. While a food truck would probably crisp up their own tortillas to make the filling, store-bought chips are the perfect trick to make these easily at home—you want to break them up roughly, but not quite crush them. We finish the tacos with a smoky, tangy sauce that you'll want to pour on everything.

1. **Make the chipotle sauce.** In a small bowl, stir together the mayonnaise, lime juice, peppers, and adobo sauce until smooth.

2. **Make the tacos.** In a medium bowl, beat together the eggs and salt.

3. Heat ½ teaspoon of the oil in a large cast-iron or nonstick skillet over medium heat. Once the oil glistens, add one tortilla and cook until toasty and warmed, about 30 seconds per side. Repeat with the remaining tortillas, adding ½ teaspoon oil to the skillet for each. Stack the toasted tortillas and wrap them in a clean kitchen towel to keep them warm.

4. Increase the heat to medium-high. Add the remaining 1 tablespoon oil to the same skillet and swirl to coat the pan. Add the broken chips and cook, stirring, until beginning to brown, 1 to 2 minutes. Reduce the heat to low and pour the beaten eggs over the chips. Let stand until barely beginning to set, about 15 seconds, then add the pico de gallo and stir slowly to scramble together the ingredients until the eggs are just set but still wet, 1 to 2 minutes. Sprinkle the shredded cheese over the top and fold a few more times until the cheese begins to melt, about 1 minute. Remove the skillet from the heat and divide the egg mixture equally among the toasted tortillas.

5. To serve, top each taco with cilantro leaves and sliced avocado. Drizzle the chipotle sauce over the top.

CRISPY GINGER RAMEN NOODLES

Serves 4
Prep Time: 12 minutes
Cook Time: 15 minutes
<35 Minutes
Dairy-Free

While we like to think we're pretty good at being grown-ups, we definitely have a few habits left over from our youth that we can't quite kick. One of them is our affection for those cheap little rectangles of dried, curlicue noodles. That said, though, we always toss that sodium-laden seasoning packet and hit the pantry. We keep a stock of a variety of sauces and seasonings in there, and we think you should, too: They're the key to many a quick, flavorful meal, including this one. Top these crispy, salty, spicy noodles with any kind of egg you like. Something about late nights and noodles just works, but this masterpiece is perfect any time.

1. Bring a large pot of water to a boil over high heat. Cook the ramen according to the package directions. Drain and set aside.

2. In a small bowl, whisk together the oyster sauce, soy sauce, rice vinegar, sesame oil, sambal oelek, garlic, and ginger.

3. Heat a large nonstick skillet over medium heat. Add the cooked ramen and sauce and toss to coat. Cook undisturbed until the noodles begin to caramelize, about 4 minutes. Using a spatula, flip the noodles over, taking care not to separate them too much. Scatter the cabbage and green onions on top and cook undisturbed until the noodles are crispy, about 4 more minutes. Toss the noodles and cabbage to combine. Cook until the cabbage just begins to wilt, about another 2 minutes.

4. Divide the noodles and vegetables among 4 plates. Top with the eggs and garnish with the sesame seeds before serving.

2 (3-ounce) packages ramen, seasoning packets discarded

2 tablespoons oyster sauce

1 tablespoon soy sauce

2 teaspoons rice vinegar

2 teaspoons toasted sesame oil

½ teaspoon sambal oelek or sriracha

4 garlic cloves, minced

1 teaspoon grated peeled fresh ginger

2 cups shredded green cabbage (about 6 ounces)

3 or 4 green onions, white and green parts, thinly sliced

4 large eggs, cooked to your liking

1 teaspoon sesame seeds

Serves 4
Prep Time: 5 Minutes
Cook Time: 10 Minutes
<35 Minutes
Gluten-Free
Kid-Friendly
Vegetarian

SMASHED SOFT-BOILED EGGS ON TOAST

Sometimes comfort looks like a vat of complicated red sauce simmering all day. But for us, most often, comfort is found in absolute simplicity: The golden yolk of a just-cooked egg, smashed up with melted butter and lifted by a handful of whatever herbs are freshest right at the moment. Mound that sunny mixture onto a slab of toast, and you're looking at a deeply soul-satisfying meal that speaks to the greatness that can be achieved with just a couple of terrific (not to mention downright inexpensive) ingredients. A lightly dressed arugula salad makes a spicy contrast and reminds us that these buttery eggs aren't just for the breakfast table—they go just as well with a glass of Champagne as they do a cup of coffee.

6 large eggs

2 tablespoons unsalted butter, melted

1 tablespoon chopped fresh chives, basil, and/or flat-leaf parsley, plus more for serving

½ teaspoon kosher salt

¼ teaspoon freshly cracked black pepper, plus more for serving

4 slices bread, toasted

Simple Arugula Salad (recipe follows)

1. Follow the instructions for making Soft-Boiled Eggs on page 32, but remove the eggs from the ice bath after 2 minutes. Immediately peel the eggs and transfer them to a medium bowl. Using a fork, smash the eggs into small pieces. Add the melted butter along with the herbs, salt, and pepper. Stir to combine until saucy.

2. Spoon the egg mixture on top of the toasted bread, dividing evenly. Season with more pepper and sprinkle with more herbs. Serve with the arugula salad alongside.

Simple Arugula Salad

SERVES 4

3 cups loosely packed arugula
2 tablespoons extra-virgin olive oil
1 tablespoon fresh lemon juice (from 1 lemon)
¼ teaspoon kosher salt
¼ teaspoon freshly cracked black pepper

In a medium bowl, toss together the arugula, olive oil, lemon juice, salt, and pepper.

BAKED EGGS
WITH GREEN OLIVES
AND FETA

Serves 4
Prep Time: 10 Minutes
Cook Time: 30 Minutes

This one is for all of you out there who, like us, crave salty over sweet in the morning. Olives, feta, and bacon all make this dish absolutely sing with bold flavors. Baked in a deeply savory mixture of cream, chard, and all the other aforementioned good stuff, the humble egg goes from everyday staple to absolute luxury. Sprinkle some toasted panko over the top to give the whole thing a textural punch, and you're done. No sugar crash to follow, but all the flavor, heartiness, and satisfaction you love about a brunch done right. Pair it simply with good coffee and crusty bread for sopping up every last droplet of those dregs.

1. Preheat the oven to 425°F with a rack in the center position.

2. Place the bacon in a medium ovenproof skillet. Set the skillet over medium heat and cook, stirring occasionally, until the bacon crisps and the fat is rendered, 5 to 7 minutes. Using a slotted spoon, transfer the bacon to a paper towel–lined plate, reserving the fat in the pan.

3. Add the onion to the bacon fat and cook, using a wooden spoon to scrape any browned bits from the bottom, until softened and translucent, about 5 minutes. Add the garlic and half of the chard and cook, stirring occasionally, until the chard is wilted, then add the remaining chard to wilt, about 2 minutes total. Return the crispy bacon to the pan and add half the olives. Remove the skillet from the heat.

4. Using a spoon, create four wells in the chard mixture. Crack one egg into each well, one at a time. Pour the cream over the entire dish.

5. Bake until the egg whites are no longer transparent, 10 to 12 minutes.

6. Meanwhile, melt the butter in a small skillet over medium heat. Add the panko and cook, stirring to coat, until toasted, about 2 minutes.

7. Sprinkle the toasted panko all over the baked eggs. Add the feta, the remaining olives, the chives, pepper, and flaky salt. Serve with crusty bread alongside.

4 slices thick-cut bacon, chopped

½ small yellow onion, diced

4 garlic cloves, minced

4 cups chopped Swiss chard leaves

½ cup pitted Castelvetrano olives, halved

4 large eggs

⅔ cup heavy cream

1 tablespoon unsalted butter

¼ cup panko breadcrumbs

¼ cup crumbled feta cheese

2 tablespoons minced fresh chives

¼ teaspoon freshly cracked black pepper

Flaky salt

Crusty bread, for serving

Serves 2
Prep Time: 15 Minutes
Cook Time: 55 Minutes
Dairy-Free
Gluten-Free
Vegetarian

JAMMY EGGS ON LENTILS WITH WILTED GREENS

French green lentils, also called lentils du puy, are a bit smaller than brown lentils. We love them because they hold their shape when cooked. Look for them in the bulk section of your favorite grocery store, or if you have trouble finding them, you can order them online easily. This preparation is pretty classic—garlic, thyme, and butter season the lentils. After you pull them from the heat, stir in even more fresh herbs. Top them with a perfectly soft-boiled egg and serve the whole, beautiful thing on a toasted baguette. We could mention that this happens to be a really high-protein vegetarian meal, but we'd rather tell you it's really delicious.

4 tablespoons (½ stick) unsalted butter or extra-virgin olive oil

2 garlic cloves, minced

1 teaspoon dried thyme leaves

½ cup French green lentils

1 teaspoon kosher salt

4 cups chopped Swiss chard leaves

1 tablespoon roughly chopped fresh tarragon leaves

2 tablespoons roughly chopped fresh chives, plus more for garnish

1 (12-inch) baguette, halved lengthwise

2 Soft-Boiled Eggs (page 32)

Flaky salt

1. Melt 2 tablespoons of the butter in a large pot with a lid over medium heat. Add the garlic and thyme and cook, stirring, until fragrant, about 1 minute. Add 3 cups water. Increase the heat to high and bring to a boil. Stir in the lentils and kosher salt, then reduce the heat to medium-low and cook, partially covered, until the lentils are mostly tender, about 45 minutes.

2. Stir in the chard, cover the pot completely, and cook until the water has been absorbed and the chard is wilted, about 4 more minutes. Remove the pot from the heat. Gently fold in the tarragon and chives.

3. Turn the oven on to broil with a rack in the center position.

4. Spread the remaining 2 tablespoons butter onto the cut sides of the baguette. Arrange the bread cut side up on a rimmed sheet pan and broil for 1 to 2 minutes, until golden brown. Cut the pieces of bread in half and set 2 slices on each plate.

5. Divide the lentils over the toasted bread. Halve the soft-boiled eggs and place one half on each piece of bread.

6. Sprinkle with flaky salt and more chives before serving.

SWEET AND SAVORY BREAKFAST SANDWICH

Makes 1 sandwich
Prep Time: 10 Minutes
Cook Time: 5 Minutes
<35 Minutes

In the early days of The Modern Proper, we entered a contest hosted by a small gourmet foods purveyor. The rules were simple: Use their wares to create the very best recipe you possibly could, and the winner would receive a $250 gift card to their shop. We got in the kitchen and dreamt up the most overindulgent breakfast sandwich we could imagine . . . Homemade buttermilk chive biscuits slathered with curry mustard, gently folded eggs—think somewhere between a plain omelette and scrambled—wild boar bacon, microgreens, and a drizzle of honey. Yeah, we won. But we also created a monster—a sandwich we craved all the time. Even with that prize money, we are just not people who keep wild boar bacon on hand. So we made some adjustments to bring the sandwich back down to earth. This simplified version is no less extra, but it's a lot easier to make anytime the mood strikes. Which, if you're anything like us, will be quite often.

1. Make the sauce. In a small bowl, stir together the mustard, mayonnaise, honey, and curry powder until combined.

2. Make the sandwich. Melt 1 tablespoon of the butter in a medium nonstick skillet over medium-high heat. Add the English muffin halves cut side down and cook, pressing down lightly, until golden brown, about 3 minutes. Transfer to a plate.

3. Wipe out the skillet and return it to medium-low heat. Add the remaining 1 tablespoon butter. In a small bowl, beat the eggs with the salt and pepper to taste. Once the butter is melted, pour in the eggs. Cook, using a heatproof rubber spatula to lift the edges and tilting the skillet to let the uncooked egg run underneath, until the eggs are mostly set but still slightly runny on top, about 2 minutes. Fold the eggs over in thirds one way then in thirds again the other way to make a stack.

4. Spread the sauce on the toasted side of both halves of the English muffin, dividing evenly. Add the eggs on the bottom and top them with the bacon, then the arugula. Finish with the top half of the English muffin. Serve immediately.

CURRY MUSTARD SAUCE
2 teaspoons stone-ground mustard

2 teaspoons mayonnaise

1 tablespoon honey

¼ teaspoon curry powder

SANDWICH
2 tablespoons salted butter

1 English muffin or brioche bun, halved

2 large eggs

¼ teaspoon fine sea salt

Freshly cracked black pepper

1 to 2 slices cooked, thick-cut bacon, cut in half (see Note)

¼ cup loosely packed arugula or microgreens

Note: When it comes to bacon, remember that low and slow yields crispy and crunchy. Always start with a cold pan. Lay down the strips, then turn the heat on low. The bacon will begin to release some of its fat, and when it starts to curl, use tongs to flip. Keep flipping and turning the bacon so it browns evenly, then remove and let cool slightly to crisp.

Serves 4 to 6
Prep Time: 15 Minutes
Cook Time: 30 Minutes
Dairy-Free
Gluten-Free
Vegetarian

CURRY POACHED EGGS

If you know us at all, you probably know we're obsessed with all things curry. You may also know we've never, ever met a baked egg dish we didn't love. It was only a matter of time before we put two and two together and this sumptuous recipe came into being. It has echoes of shakshuka, the classic North African dish of eggs baked in a saucy, spicy mixture of tomatoes and peppers. And we've taken those wonderful, rich flavors and built on them, adding yellow curry powder for extra complexity and coconut milk for creamy balance. It may take a bit of practice to get the eggs just right—you want runny yolks, but set whites. Our best advice is to simply watch the pan carefully and pull it as soon as those whites look set.

1 tablespoon extra-virgin olive oil

1 small yellow onion, diced

2 garlic cloves, roughly chopped

1 (14.5-ounce) can diced tomatoes

2 tablespoons yellow curry powder

1 teaspoon ground cinnamon

1 teaspoon ground cumin

½ teaspoon fine sea salt

1 (13.5-ounce) can full-fat coconut milk, shaken

2 large red bell peppers, thinly sliced

1 (15-ounce) can chickpeas, drained and rinsed

4 to 6 large eggs

Fresh cilantro, for garnish (optional)

Flatbread, for serving (optional)

1. Heat the olive oil in a large skillet over medium heat. Once the oil is glistening, add the onion and cook, stirring occasionally, until softened and translucent, about 5 minutes. Add the garlic and continue cooking until fragrant, about 1 more minute. Add the diced tomatoes and their juices, the curry powder, cinnamon, cumin, and salt and stir to combine. Slowly stir in the coconut milk and bring to a simmer. Cook, stirring often, until the flavors are melded, about 5 minutes. Remove the skillet from the heat.

2. Use an immersion blender to blend the liquid directly in the skillet. (Alternatively, transfer the liquid to the base of a blender, let cool briefly, and blend until smooth. Then return it to the skillet.) Bring the curry to a simmer over medium heat. Add the bell peppers. Cook, stirring occasionally, until the peppers are beginning to soften, about 8 minutes. Stir in the chickpeas.

3. Reduce the heat to medium-low. Gently crack the eggs into the curry sauce. Cook until the whites are set, 5 to 8 minutes. Garnish with cilantro and serve family-style with flatbread alongside, if desired.

EGGS WITH CRISPY GREEN ONION RICE AND NORI

Serves 2
Prep Time: 10 Minutes
Cook Time: 5 Minutes
<35 Minutes
Dairy-Free
Gluten-Free
Vegetarian

If you have rice left over from last night's takeout—and we always seem to have a carton lurking in the fridge—don't toss it! Use it to make this garlicky, seaweed-flecked fried rice bowl instead. Any kind of rice will work, and most any kind of Asian chili sauce will work, too. We especially love chili crisp—and for its texture as much as for its flavor. This Chinese condiment is made with dried chili flakes that are fried, creating a satisfying crunch. It's a fun way to dress up this simple meal, but it's also totally optional. Use what you have, and use what you like!

1. In a medium bowl, toss together the cooked rice, green onions, and nori. Season to taste with salt.

2. Heat the vegetable oil in a large skillet over high heat. Once the oil is glistening, add the garlic and cook, stirring, until fragrant, about 30 seconds. Add the rice mixture and stir a few times to coat with the oil. Press the rice evenly across the bottom of the skillet. Cook, undisturbed, until the bottom of the rice begins to turn golden brown, 3 to 4 minutes.

3. Spoon the rice out of the pan, dividing it evenly between 2 plates. Top each with an egg. Add toppings as desired and serve.

2 cups cooked rice, preferably day-old

4 green onions, white and green parts, chopped

1 sheet nori, cut into thin strips

Fine sea salt

2 tablespoons vegetable oil

1 garlic clove, minced

2 large eggs, cooked to your liking

FOR SERVING
Chili crisp

Sliced cucumber

Low-sodium soy sauce, tamari, or coconut aminos (see Note on page 156)

Sriracha

Sesame seeds

Serves 4
Prep Time: 15 to 30 Minutes
Cook Time: 15 to 30 Minutes
Dairy-Free
Gluten-Free
Vegetarian

ANY ROASTED VEGGIE WITH ROMESCO SAUCE

If you want to roast a vegetable so it's truly tender on the inside and just slightly charred on the outside, you must have high heat. 425°F is our roasting temperature of choice for all vegetables. All you need to know is that number—425—and the respective cook time for various veggies. Some, like asparagus or green beans, take almost no time. Potatoes, on the other hand, take a little longer. That said, you can still roast them all together on one pan! You'll just need to work those elementary school math skills. Load your sheet pan with the vegetables that take longer first and pop it in the oven. Add the other vegetables at the appropriate intervals until suddenly you have a pan of perfectly cooked veggies of all kinds. Two tips: Go easy on the oil (too much will make everything soggy), and make sure the vegetables aren't touching.

1 pound vegetables of your choice (see chart below)

2 tablespoons extra-virgin olive oil

¾ teaspoon kosher salt

Romesco Sauce (page 275)

1. Preheat the oven to 425°F with a rack in the center position.

2. In a medium bowl, toss the vegetables with the olive oil and salt. Arrange the vegetables on a rimmed sheet pan, being careful not to overcrowd (see Note on page 170). Roast, according to the guidelines below, until the vegetables are browned and tender.

3. Transfer the vegetables to a serving platter. Serve with the Romesco alongside for dipping.

VEGETABLE	PREPARATION	ROASTING TIME
Acorn squash	seeds removed, cut into ½-inch-thick rings	20 minutes
Asparagus	trimmed	10 to 12 minutes
Bell pepper	cut into ½-inch-thick strips	20 minutes; flip after 10 minutes
Broccoli	cut into florets	20 minutes
Brussels sprouts	halved or quartered if large	20 minutes; cut side down
Butternut squash	cut into 1-inch cubes	30 minutes
Carrots	peeled and halved lengthwise	15 to 20 minutes; cut side down
Cauliflower	cut into florets	30 minutes
Eggplant	cut into 1-inch cubes	25 to 30 minutes
Green beans	trimmed	15 minutes
Onion	cut into ½-inch wedges	20 minutes; flip after 10 minutes
New potatoes	halved	20 minutes; cut side down
Sweet potato	cut into 1-inch cubes	25 to 30 minutes
Summer squash	cut into ½-inch-thick slices	20 minutes; flip after 10 minutes
Zucchini	cut into ½-inch-thick slices	20 to 25 minutes; flip after 10 minutes

STUFFED PORTOBELLO MUSHROOMS

Serves 4 to 6
Prep Time: 20 Minutes
Cook Time: 25 Minutes
Gluten-Free
Vegetarian

Usually when you're stuffing something, the bigger the vessel the better. Stuffed shells, peppers, cannoli . . . and definitely these stuffed mushrooms. You'll want to pick out the largest portobellos you can find, as they'll shrink a bit and flatten out in the oven. Look for ones with a nice, deep well to fill with the garlicky feta-spinach mixture. We'll begin by snapping off their stems, but don't worry—we'd never waste that shroomy goodness. Stirred back into the stuffing, it links the filling to the portobello cap, making this dish nutty, earthy, and so mouthwatering.

1. Preheat the oven to 350°F.

2. Remove the mushroom stems from the caps. Roughly chop the stems.

3. Spread 2 tablespoons of the olive oil in a small roasting pan or baking dish. Add the mushroom caps, rounded side down. Brush the insides of the mushrooms with another 2 tablespoons of the oil and sprinkle with 1 teaspoon of the salt. Bake for 25 minutes, or until tender.

4. Meanwhile, heat the remaining 1 tablespoon oil in a large skillet over medium heat. Once the oil is glistening, add the chopped mushroom stems, walnuts, red onion, asparagus, garlic, and herbs. Cook, stirring occasionally, until the asparagus is vibrant and tender and the onion is softened, about 3 minutes. Add the spinach and brown rice and season with the remaining ½ teaspoon salt and the pepper. Cook, stirring occasionally, until the spinach is wilted, about 3 minutes.

5. Spoon the brown rice mixture into the roasted mushroom caps, dividing evenly. Top with feta and serve.

6 large portobello mushrooms

5 tablespoons extra-virgin olive oil

1½ teaspoons kosher salt

⅓ cup roughly chopped walnuts

½ small red onion, minced

4 asparagus spears, ends trimmed, cut into 1-inch pieces

2 garlic cloves, minced

2 tablespoons minced fresh herbs, such as thyme, chives, flat-leaf parsley, or basil

4 cups loosely packed baby spinach

1½ cups cooked brown rice, farro, or barley

¼ teaspoon freshly cracked black pepper

2 ounces feta cheese, crumbled

Serves 10

Prep Time: 10 Minutes

Cook Time: 20 Minutes

<35 Minutes

Kid-Friendly

Vegetarian

CHEESY TAMALE PIE WITH QUINOA AND BEAN CHILI

Tamale pie is often a beefy affair. But we've found that between the slightly sweet, buttery cornbread, hearty quinoa-bean chili, and mountain of cheese, this homey casserole just doesn't need the meat. Plus, leaving it out makes this crowd-favorite meal more accessible to more people, which is always a good thing. If you're lucky enough to have any leftovers—if you're feeding a small group, then you will—rejoice! It's just as lovable the next day.

CORNBREAD

Cooking spray

1⅓ cups all-purpose flour

1 cup yellow cornmeal

¼ cup sugar

1 tablespoon baking powder

½ teaspoon baking soda

½ teaspoon kosher salt

1 (14.75-ounce) can creamed corn

½ cup (1 stick) melted salted butter, cooled slightly

½ cup sour cream

2 large eggs, beaten

TOPPING

1 tablespoon extra-virgin olive oil

1 cup chopped yellow onion (from 1 medium onion)

1 red bell pepper, chopped

1 (15-ounce) can black beans, drained and rinsed

1 (15-ounce) can crushed tomatoes

1 (28-ounce) can red enchilada sauce

2 tablespoons Taco Seasoning (page 267)

1½ cups cooked quinoa

2½ cups shredded cheddar cheese

1. **Make the cornbread.** Preheat the oven to 400°F with a rack in the center position. Grease a 12-inch cast-iron skillet or 9 x 13-inch baking dish with cooking spray.

2. In a medium bowl, whisk together the flour, cornmeal, sugar, baking powder, baking soda, and salt. In a large bowl, stir together the creamed corn, butter, sour cream, and eggs. Slowly add the dry ingredients to the wet ingredients, stirring until just combined. Do not overmix.

3. Pour the batter into the prepared skillet and bake for about 15 minutes, or until a tester inserted into the center of the cornbread comes out clean.

4. **Meanwhile, make the topping.** Heat the olive oil in a large skillet over medium heat. Once the oil is glistening, add the onion and bell pepper and cook, stirring occasionally, until softened, about 5 minutes. Stir in the beans, tomatoes, half of the enchilada sauce, and the taco seasoning. Cook, stirring often, until the mixture begins to thicken, about 10 minutes. Stir in the quinoa and 1 cup of the cheese.

5. Remove the cornbread from the oven and turn on the broiler. Using the handle of a wooden spoon, poke several holes in the cornbread. Pour the remaining enchilada sauce over the top. Add the quinoa mixture, spread it into an even layer, and sprinkle the remaining 1½ cups cheese all over. Return the skillet to the oven and broil until the cheese is melted and bubbly, 3 to 4 minutes.

6. Scoop the tamale pie onto plates to serve.

Serves 4
Prep Time: 5 Minutes
Cook Time: 20 Minutes
<35 Minutes
Vegetarian

When is toast so much more than toast? When you make it with slices of crusty bread, pan-frying them to rich, golden goodness in olive oil. Sprinkle on a little salt, but don't stop there. Take that already-fabulous blank slate and start piling on—your toast is ready to serve as a sturdy base for almost anything. You'd be surprised how easily you can turn a single piece of bread into a kinda-fancy dinner by simply exploring the odds and ends in your cheese and produce drawers, not to mention the far reaches of your cupboards. We say get creative! If there's a combination of mish-mashed ingredients that sounds good to you, pile it on some toast and call it dinner! That said, if you need a little inspiration to get started, we've got you covered. From lemony ricotta with greens to a totally luxe mushroom cream sauce, you'll find plenty of fuel for creating your own toast-centric meals here.

4 tablespoons extra-virgin olive oil

4 slices thick crusty bread

¼ teaspoon flaky salt

1. Heat 2 tablespoons of the olive oil in a large skillet over medium-high heat. Once the oil is glistening, add the bread. Cook until golden brown and crisp on the bottom, about 5 minutes. Remove the bread from the skillet. Add the remaining 2 tablespoons oil to coat the bottom of the pan. Return the bread to the skillet and cook until golden and crisp on the other side, about another 5 minutes.

2. Transfer the bread to a plate. Sprinkle with the salt, dividing evenly.

Makes 2 cups

MUSHROOM SAUCE

16 ounces cremini mushrooms, ends trimmed, quartered

½ teaspoon fine sea salt

2 tablespoons unsalted butter

1 cup heavy cream

2 tablespoon low-sodium soy sauce or tamari

2 tablespoons fresh thyme leaves

1. In a large nonstick skillet over medium heat, arrange the mushrooms in a single layer. Cook, undisturbed, until beginning to brown, 3 to 5 minutes. Add the salt, give the mushrooms a stir, and cook until their liquid releases, about 5 minutes. Continue cooking, stirring, until tender, about another 2 minutes.

2. Add the butter and cook until it melts and begins to bubble. Stir in the cream, soy sauce, and thyme. Bring the sauce to a low simmer. Cook, stirring constantly, until thickened, 3 to 4 minutes. Spoon the sauce over the toast, dividing evenly.

GARLICKY SAUTÉED KALE & LEMON RICOTTA

Makes 1½ cups

1. Heat the olive oil in a large skillet over medium heat. Once the oil is glistening, add the kale, garlic, and ¼ teaspoon of the fine salt. Cook, stirring occasionally, until the kale is wilted, about 8 minutes.

2. Meanwhile, in a small bowl, stir together the ricotta, lemon zest, the remaining ¼ teaspoon fine salt, and the pepper to combine.

3. Spread the ricotta mixture over the toast, dividing evenly. Top with the sautéed kale. Sprinkle with flaky salt to taste.

2 tablespoons extra-virgin olive oil

4 cups loosely packed stemmed and roughly chopped curly kale

2 garlic cloves, minced

½ teaspoon fine sea salt

½ cup whole-milk ricotta

1 teaspoon grated lemon zest

¼ teaspoon freshly cracked black pepper

Flaky salt

BRAISED CHICKPEAS

Makes 2⅓ cups

1. Heat the olive oil in a large skillet over medium heat. Once the oil is glistening, add the chickpeas and cook, stirring occasionally, until just beginning to brown, about 4 minutes. Add the garlic and paprika. Cook, stirring, until fragrant, about 2 more minutes.

2. Pour in the marinara and cook, stirring, until the sauce begins to thicken, about 10 minutes. Add the greens and stir until just wilted, about 2 minutes.

3. Spoon the mixture over the toast, dividing evenly.

¼ cup extra-virgin olive oil or unsalted butter

1 (15-ounce) can chickpeas, drained and rinsed

4 garlic cloves, thinly sliced

1 tablespoon smoked paprika

1 (24-ounce) jar marinara sauce

2 cups finely chopped stemmed Swiss chard leaves or curly kale (about 6 ounces)

TOAST FOR DINNER

Braised Chickpeas, *page 63*

Garlicky Sautéed Kale
& Lemon Ricotta, *page 63*

Mushroom Sauce, *page 62*

ROASTED SWEET POTATOES WITH LABNEH AND HONEY

Serves 4

Prep Time: 5 Minutes, plus time to strain

Cook Time: 45 Minutes

Gluten-Free

Vegetarian

Did you ever have a baked potato for dinner when you were a kid? We did. With a little bit of thought, even the humblest ingredient can reach great heights. Turns out sweet potatoes are no different, and we've proved it. The simple swap—replacing russet potatoes with sweet potatoes—makes for a major upgrade, both visually and nutritionally. Top these golden beauts with homemade labneh, a thick and tangy Middle Eastern yogurt made by straining Greek yogurt. You can have it ready to use in about an hour, but if you plan ahead a bit, the labneh will be even better strained overnight.

1. Set a strainer over a large bowl. Place the yogurt in a cheesecloth, nut bag, or tea towel, and set on top of the strainer. Let the yogurt sit, refrigerated, until most of the liquid is strained out, at least 1 hour or up to overnight. The longer you leave it, the thicker the labneh will be.

2. Preheat the oven to 425°F with a rack in the center position. Line a rimmed sheet pan with parchment.

3. Prick each sweet potato 6 or 7 times with a fork, then arrange them on the prepared sheet pan. Bake until tender, about 45 minutes. Let cool for about 5 minutes.

4. In a small, heatproof bowl, stir together the honey, cinnamon, and ginger. Heat the spiced honey in the microwave on high in 10-second intervals, stirring in between, for 30 seconds total.

5. Using a sharp knife, slit the tops of the potatoes open and fluff the insides with a fork. Top each potato with a generous dollop of labneh, a drizzle of spiced honey, and the crushed pistachios, dividing evenly. Sprinkle with flaky salt before serving.

¾ cup plain Greek yogurt

4 small sweet potatoes (about 1 pound)

⅓ cup honey

1½ teaspoons ground cinnamon

1½ teaspoons ground ginger

¼ cup coarsely chopped raw pistachios

Flaky salt, for serving

Serves 4
Prep Time: 20 Minutes
Cook Time: 40 Minutes
Gluten-Free
Sheet Pan
Vegetarian

TOFU ENCHILADAS
WITH RED SAUCE

When you think of enchiladas, you probably think of a casserole, but what if we told you there's another way? All you need is a sheet pan and some toothpicks. Inspired by a dish you might find in Oaxaca, this recipe delivers all of the saucy, cheesy goodness that we crave when an enchilada hankering hits, minus the meat. A quick toss with our killer homemade taco seasoning, followed by a roast, brings a satisfying richness out of the tofu and zucchini. Store-bought sauce keeps this recipe firmly planted in the land of weeknight do-ability, and we've called for mozzarella, which is famous for being a fantastic melter. Cotija and red onions make the perfect finish.

1 (14-ounce) block extra-firm tofu, cut into 1-inch cubes and drained (see Note)

3 medium zucchini, halved lengthwise then cut into ¾-inch-thick slices (about 2 cups)

3 tablespoons vegetable oil, plus more as needed

2 tablespoons Taco Seasoning (page 267)

10 (6-inch) corn tortillas

10 ounces low-moisture mozzarella cheese, shredded

1 (10-ounce) can mild red enchilada sauce

¼ cup crumbled Cotija cheese, for serving

Red onions, sliced, for serving

Fresh cilantro leaves, for serving

Note: To drain tofu, cut the block into 1-inch cubes. Line a rimmed sheet pan or large plate with a double layer of paper towels. Spread out the tofu on the paper towels, and add another double layer on top of the tofu. Cover the paper towels with something heavy, like a sheet pan weighted with a cast-iron skillet. Let drain for 30 minutes.

1. Preheat the oven to 400°F.

2. Arrange the tofu and zucchini on a rimmed sheet pan. Add 2 tablespoons of the vegetable oil and the taco seasoning and toss to coat evenly. Bake for 15 minutes. Turn on the broiler and cook for another 5 to 7 minutes, until the tofu and zucchini are golden brown. Remove the sheet pan from the oven and reduce the oven temperature to 350°F.

3. Meanwhile, heat 1 teaspoon of the oil in a medium skillet over medium heat. Once the oil is glistening, add 1 tortilla and fry until just softened, about 30 seconds per side. Transfer to a paper towel–lined plate. Repeat with the remaining tortillas, adding more oil to the skillet as needed.

4. Fill each tortilla with tofu, zucchini, mozzarella, and 1 tablespoon enchilada sauce. Fold the tortillas in half, secure them with a toothpick, and arrange them on the same sheet pan, overlapping slightly. Pour the remaining enchilada sauce all over and bake until the cheese has melted, about 15 minutes.

5. Top the enchiladas with the Cotija, red onions, and cilantro before serving.

CURRIED CAULIFLOWER QUINOA SALAD WITH TAHINI YOGURT DRESSING

Serves 4
Prep Time: 15 Minutes
Cook Time: 30 Minutes
Gluten-Free
Vegetarian

If our friendship is bound by one shared philosophy, "will travel for food" just might be it. Working together means we often find ourselves hitting the road (or skies), and the opportunity to explore the food scene in a new city is one we both relish. While we've been known to gush over a deep bowl of swirly pasta, or crispy, crunchy tacos, sometimes it's a really great salad that's the standout dish of a trip. We're thinking of a particular salad we first tasted in Los Angeles—right away, we were smitten. We ordered it over and over, and once we were back home, we set out to re-create it and make it our own. The florets of roasted, curried cauliflower against the tangy tahini, lemon, and yogurt dressing are captivating, and the sweet golden raisins speckled throughout keep our taste buds baited for the next bite. Sure, this salad has a few components, but isn't that a small price to pay for a healthy, gorgeous meal you'll be dreaming about for weeks to come?

1. **Make the cauliflower.** Preheat the oven to 425°F with a rack in the center position.

2. On a rimmed sheet pan, drizzle the cauliflower with the olive oil. Sprinkle on the curry powder and salt and toss to coat. Spread out the cauliflower in a single layer. Bake for 30 minutes, or until golden brown and tender.

3. **Meanwhile, make the dressing.** In the base of a blender or food processor, combine the cucumber, yogurt, tahini, lemon juice, oil, garlic, and salt. Blend until smooth, about 2 minutes.

4. **Make the salad.** In a large bowl, toss together the arugula, quinoa, and cabbage. Divide the mixture among 4 bowls. Top each with the roasted cauliflower, cucumbers, cilantro, and raisins. Drizzle the dressing over the top and serve.

CAULIFLOWER

1½ pounds cauliflower, cut into small florets

¼ cup extra-virgin olive oil

2 tablespoons curry powder

2 teaspoons fine sea salt

DRESSING

1 cup roughly chopped Persian cucumber (from 2 cucumbers)

½ cup plain Greek yogurt

⅓ cup tahini

⅓ cup fresh lemon juice (from 3 lemons)

2 tablespoons extra-virgin olive oil

1 garlic clove, roughly chopped

½ teaspoon fine sea salt

SALAD

4 cups loosely packed arugula

2 cups cooked quinoa, room temperature

2 cups shredded red cabbage (about 6 ounces)

2 Persian cucumbers, diced

¼ cup fresh cilantro leaves

⅓ cup golden raisins

Serves 4
Prep Time: 10 Minutes
Cook Time: 25 Minutes
<35 Minutes
Vegetarian

SAUCY GRILLED CHEESE WITH ASPARAGUS

Low and slow is the name of our grilled cheese game. Whatever you do, don't try to rush yours. It cannot be done without compromising the perfectly golden crunch of this toasty meal. Much like the use of Gruyère and fancy bread, the addition of asparagus is because we're grown-ups now, and dare we say it improves the gooey goodness of a cheese sandwich by adding a little more interest and a hint of vegetable bite that cuts through all that dairy fat. Nutty and smoky, with a nice acidic bite, Romesco sauce is likewise a perfect foil for all of the richness at play here. We suggest serving the extra sauce alongside the sandwich for dipping.

½ pound pencil-thin asparagus, ends trimmed, cut into 4-inch pieces

1 tablespoon extra-virgin olive oil

½ teaspoon kosher salt

¼ teaspoon freshly cracked black pepper

4 tablespoons mayonnaise

4 tablespoons (½ stick) salted butter, softened

8 slices ciabatta or other rustic bread

1¾ cups Romesco Sauce (page 275)

6 ounces grated Gruyère cheese, room temperature

6 ounces thinly sliced fresh mozzarella cheese, room temperature

1. Preheat the oven to 400°F with a rack in the center position.

2. On a rimmed sheet pan, combine the asparagus, olive oil, salt, and pepper. Toss to combine, then spread out the asparagus. Bake for 10 minutes, or until tender and starting to brown.

3. In a small bowl, stir together the mayonnaise and butter. Spread the mixture on one side of each slice of bread. Spread about 1 tablespoon of the Romesco on the other side of each of 4 pieces of the bread, then layer on the Gruyère, asparagus, and mozzarella, dividing evenly. Finish the sandwiches with the remaining slices of bread, buttered side facing out.

4. Heat a large cast-iron skillet or griddle over low heat. Add two sandwiches at a time and cook, watching closely, until golden brown on the bottom, about 8 minutes. Flip and repeat on the other side.

5. Transfer the sandwiches to plates and serve with the remaining Romesco alongside for dipping.

CHARRED SUMMER SQUASH WITH WHIPPED FETA

Serves 4
Prep Time: 15 Minutes
Cook Time: 20 Minutes
<35 minutes
Gluten-Free
Vegetarian

You'd be hard-pressed to find something that doesn't go well with this tangy, fresh feta dip. Whipped together with cream cheese and a handful of herbs, it's nothing short of divine—we could eat it with a peeled carrot and be happy campers. However, if you really want to achieve a state of culinary rapture, sauté some tender summer squash and chickpeas in smoky paprika and pair the golden mixture with this cloudlike fluff of feta. Rip off pieces of warm naan (or another flatbread of your choosing) and dredge at will.

1. In the base of a food processor, combine the feta, cream cheese, chives, rosemary, thyme, and black pepper. Blend on high speed until smooth, 1 to 2 minutes. Spread the whipped feta onto a serving platter.

2. In a small bowl, stir together the olive oil, paprika, granulated garlic, salt, and cayenne. In a medium bowl, combine the zucchini with half of the spiced oil and toss to coat.

3. Heat a large skillet over medium heat. Working in batches as needed, add the zucchini in a single layer. Cook, undisturbed, until brown and crispy on the edges, about 4 minutes. Flip and repeat on the other side, about another 4 minutes. Carefully transfer the zucchini to the serving platter, arranging it on top of the feta.

4. Add the chickpeas and the remaining spiced oil to the same skillet over medium heat. Cook, stirring, until the chickpeas are evenly coated and warmed through, about 3 minutes. Scatter over the platter with the feta and zucchini.

5. Drizzle the platter with more olive oil and with mint, if desired. Serve with warmed naan alongside.

5 ounces feta cheese

4 ounces cream cheese, softened

1 tablespoon roughly chopped fresh chives

1 tablespoon roughly chopped fresh rosemary

1 tablespoon fresh thyme leaves

½ teaspoon freshly cracked black pepper

3 tablespoons extra-virgin olive oil, plus more for serving

2 teaspoons smoked paprika

2 teaspoons granulated garlic

½ teaspoon kosher salt

¼ teaspoon cayenne pepper

2 medium zucchini or yellow squash, cut into ½-inch-thick rounds

¾ cup canned chickpeas, drained and rinsed

Minced fresh mint leaves, for serving (optional)

Warmed naan or flatbread, for serving

Serves 4

Prep Time: 25 Minutes

Cook Time: 1 Hour 10 Minutes

Kid-Friendly

Gluten-Free

Vegetarian

STUFFED SPAGHETTI SQUASH WITH LENTIL WALNUT BOLOGNESE

We didn't exactly set out to prove that vegetarian food can be as easy and savory as its counterpart, but this recipe does exactly that. Walnuts, with their earthy flavor and unique texture, plus protein-loaded lentils, team up to make a Bolognese dupe that really hits the spot. This meaty, meatless sauce even has a nice creaminess when you blend some (but not all!) of it. In doing so, the fat from the walnuts emulsifies with the tomato sauce and lentils to give you a texture and richness that mimics classic, milk-tinged Bolognese.

1 tablespoon extra-virgin olive oil, plus more for greasing

1 large carrot, peeled and grated (about ½ cup)

1 celery rib, finely minced (about ½ cup)

½ small yellow onion, finely minced (about ½ cup)

1 (24-ounce) jar marinara sauce

½ cup finely chopped walnuts

½ cup green lentils, rinsed

2 teaspoons fine sea salt

2 medium spaghetti squash, halved lengthwise, seeds removed

2 cups shredded mozzarella cheese

Minced fresh basil leaves or flat-leaf parsley leaves, for serving

1. Preheat the oven to 425°F. Grease a rimmed sheet pan or large baking dish.

2. Heat the olive oil in a medium saucepan over medium heat. Once the oil is glistening, add the carrot, celery, and onion and cook, stirring occasionally, until softened, about 6 minutes.

3. Add 3 cups water, the marinara sauce, walnuts, lentils, and 1 teaspoon of the salt. Stir to combine. Reduce the heat to medium-low and cook, stirring occasionally, until the lentils are tender and the sauce is thickened, about 45 minutes. Use an immersion blender to blend the sauce to your desired consistency directly in the pan; it should still have some texture to it. (Alternatively, transfer 2 cups of the sauce to the base of a blender, let cool briefly, blend until nearly smooth, and then return the sauce to the pan.)

4. Meanwhile, place the squash cut side down on the prepared sheet pan. Bake for 40 minutes, or until the squash is very tender. Remove from the oven, leaving the oven on. Carefully flip the squash and using a fork, scrape the flesh to loosen the spaghetti-like strands. Season with the remaining 1 teaspoon salt.

5. Fill each piece of squash with ¼ cup shredded cheese. Add the sauce, dividing evenly. Top with the remaining cheese. Return the squash to the oven and bake for 15 more minutes, or until the cheese is golden and bubbling.

6. Remove the squash from the oven and let cool for 5 minutes. Again, using a fork, scrape deep into the squash, mixing the squash, sauce, and cheese together. Garnish with minced herbs and serve.

SPICY UNSTUFFED PASTA SHELLS WITH ROASTED GARLIC AND CHÈVRE

Serves 4
Prep Time: 10 Minutes
Cook Time: 35 Minutes
Kid-Friendly
Vegetarian

The olive bar has to be the most underrated section of the grocery store. To make the most of that little treasure trove, we like to think of the stuff we find there not only as snacks, but also as hugely flavorful, time-saving ingredients! Peppadews and marinated feta are great, but we never walk past without stocking up on roasted garlic. The soft, sweet, subtly nutty cloves that would take hours to make at home are almost always available, already cooked to perfection and ready to lend some delicate, nutty, molten garlic love to any dish they grace. They're one of just five ingredients that make this hearty pasta sauce oh-so-good with oh-so-little effort. Another trick that makes this dish work so well? Adding a bit of salty, starchy pasta cooking liquid to the pan helps in creating a creamy sauce that really clings to the shells.

1. Preheat the oven to 375°F.

2. Fill a large pot with 4 quarts water and add the salt. Bring to a boil over high heat. Add the pasta and cook for 8 minutes; it will be underdone. Reserve ¾ cup of the liquid and drain the pasta.

3. Meanwhile, in a large ovenproof skillet, combine the marinara, roasted garlic, 1 ounce of the chèvre, and the red pepper flakes. Cook over medium heat, stirring often, until the cheese is fully incorporated, about 2 minutes.

4. Add the pasta to the skillet along with the reserved cooking liquid. Cook over medium heat, stirring to combine, about 2 minutes. Dollop the remaining 3 ounces chèvre all over.

5. Bake for 15 minutes. Turn on the broiler and cook until the cheese is brown and bubbly, about 2 more minutes.

6. Top with the parsley and more red pepper flakes. Serve warm.

2 teaspoons kosher salt

12 ounces large pasta shells

1 (24-ounce) jar marinara sauce

¼ cup roasted garlic, drained and roughly chopped (see headnote)

4 ounces chèvre cheese (see Note)

½ teaspoon red pepper flakes, plus more for serving

Roughly chopped fresh flat-leaf parsley leaves, for serving

Note: If you aren't familiar with chèvre, it's also known simply as "goat cheese."

79

Serves 6
Prep Time: 15 Minutes
Cook Time: 35 Minutes
Dairy-Free
Gluten-Free
Vegetarian

LENTIL AND CHICKPEA TAGINE

Lentils are a perennial favorite in our kitchens, and for good reason. They're inexpensive and filling, and they last forever in the pantry. But somewhere along the way, our beloved legume got a reputation for being bland—and this vegan tagine is here to right that wrong. Heady spices, fresh lemon juice, and pistachios root it firmly in Morocco, where the delicious stew known as tagine was born more than a thousand years ago. While the word "tagine" is synonymous with a slow-cooked, tomatoey, heavily spiced, often sweet-savory stew, it's also the name of the conical clay pot in which the stew is traditionally cooked. If you happen to have one—great! But if not, you can use a Dutch oven to mimic the heft and moist-heat cooking environment that a true Moroccan tagine would create.

1 tablespoon extra-virgin olive oil

3 large shallots, thinly sliced

4 garlic cloves, roughly chopped

1 tablespoon minced peeled fresh ginger

2 tablespoons tomato paste

2 teaspoons kosher salt

1 teaspoon ground cumin

1 teaspoon ground turmeric

1 teaspoon ground cinnamon

1 quart vegetable stock

1 (14.5-ounce) can diced tomatoes

1½ cups green or black lentils

1 tablespoon light brown sugar

1 (15-ounce) can chickpeas, drained and rinsed

½ cup roughly chopped dried apricots

⅓ cup roughly chopped pistachios, plus more for garnish (optional)

1 tablespoon fresh lemon juice (from 1 lemon)

Cooked rice or cauliflower rice, for serving (optional)

¼ red onion, thinly sliced (optional)

¼ cup finely chopped fresh mint (optional)

1. Heat the olive oil in a large Dutch oven over medium-high heat. Once the oil is glistening, add the shallots and cook, stirring, until beginning to soften, about 3 minutes. Add the garlic and ginger and cook, stirring, until fragrant, about 1 more minute. Add the tomato paste, salt, cumin, turmeric, and cinnamon and cook, stirring, until the tomato paste is incorporated and the spices are fragrant, about 2 minutes.

2. Add the vegetable stock, 2 cups water, the tomatoes and their juices, the lentils, and the brown sugar and stir to combine. Increase the heat to high and bring to a boil, then reduce the heat to low, cover, and simmer, stirring occasionally, until the lentils are tender but not mushy, about 20 minutes. Add the chickpeas, stir to combine, and simmer until warmed through, about 5 more minutes.

3. Remove the Dutch oven from the heat. Stir in the apricots, pistachios, if desired, and lemon juice. Serve over rice or enjoy on its own. Garnish with the red onion, fresh mint, and more pistachios, if desired.

Note: For even deeper flavor, you can replace the water with more vegetable stock.

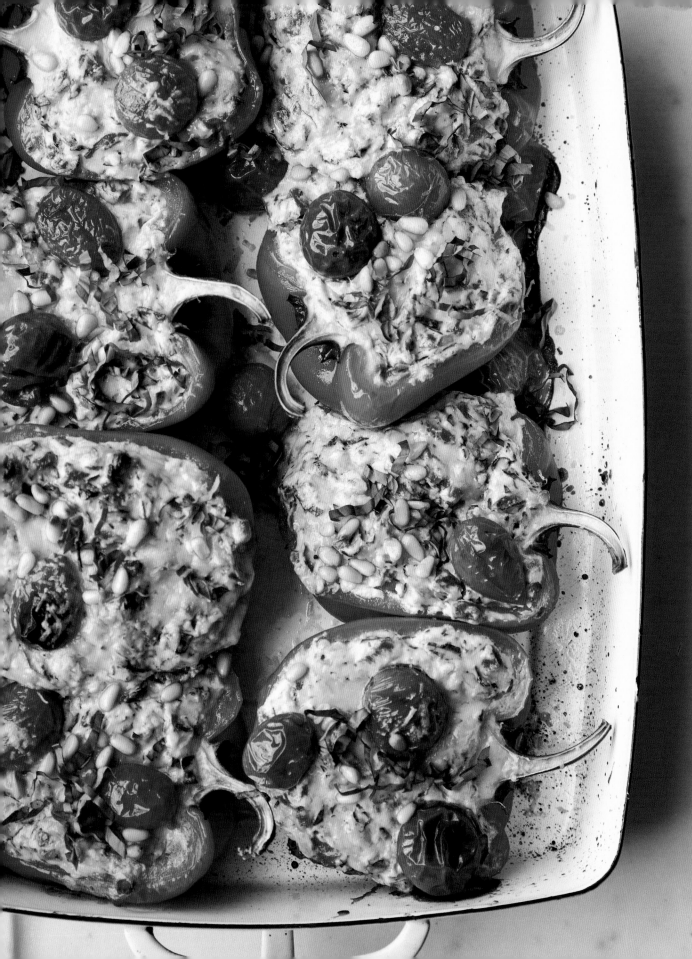

RICOTTA-STUFFED PEPPERS WITH ROASTED TOMATOES

Serves 4 to 6
Prep Time: 15 Minutes
Cook Time: 40 Minutes
Gluten-Free
Vegetarian

Just like it would be impossible to claim that our moms' chicken noodle soup is actually the best on the planet, we're not going to bother claiming these are the very best stuffed peppers ever because we know you probably have deep loyalty to the version you grew up with. So, let's just say these are pretty great, okay? We took our favorite Italian flavors—basil, Parmesan, pine nuts, and ricotta—and used them to perk up a super basic stuffed pepper dinner that might just be the best ever (but you didn't hear that from us).

1. Preheat the oven to 400°F. Grease a 9 x 13-inch baking dish with olive oil.

2. In a large bowl, combine the ricotta, mozzarella, roasted red peppers, spinach, eggs, Italian seasoning, and 1 teaspoon of the salt. Stir to mix well.

3. Halve the bell peppers lengthwise, keeping the stems intact as much as possible. Discard the seeds and ribs. Arrange the peppers in the prepared baking dish and fill them with the ricotta mixture, dividing evenly.

4. In a medium bowl, toss the tomatoes with the 2 tablespoons olive oil and the remaining ½ teaspoon salt. Scatter the tomatoes over the peppers.

5. Bake for 30 minutes. Remove from the oven and sprinkle the stuffed peppers with the Parmesan and pine nuts. Return to the oven and continue baking for another 8 to 10 minutes, or until the ricotta is set and the pine nuts are toasted.

6. Sprinkle with the fresh basil, if desired, and more Parmesan. Serve family-style.

2 tablespoons extra-virgin olive oil, plus more for greasing

15 ounces whole-milk ricotta

1½ cups shredded mozzarella cheese

1 (12-ounce) jar roasted red peppers, drained, chopped, and squeezed dry

2 cups loosely packed baby spinach, chopped

2 large eggs

2 teaspoons Italian seasoning

1½ teaspoons fine sea salt

4 large red bell peppers

1 pint cherry tomatoes

¼ cup freshly grated Parmesan cheese, plus more for serving

¼ cup pine nuts

¼ cup finely chopped fresh basil leaves, for serving (optional)

Serves 2 to 4

Prep Time: 5 Minutes

Cook Time: 15 Minutes

<35 Minutes

Gluten-Free

Kid-Friendly

Vegetarian

CLEAN-OUT-THE-PANTRY PASTA

Exactly what it sounds like, this recipe is our trusty go-to for whenever we need to make a quick meal out of whatever we can dig out from the back of the cupboard. Think of it as a blank slate: an incredibly easy, creamy, cheesy base that plays well with others. It truly works with any kind of pasta you have on hand—and while we've suggested some of our favorite add-in combinations, you should have fun with it! Whether you stir in two things or ten, this recipe is all about using what you've got—and a testament to the fact that necessity is the mother of invention. The more you mix in, the more mouths it will feed.

2¼ teaspoons fine sea salt

8 ounces pasta of your choice

4 tablespoons (½ stick) unsalted butter

⅔ cup freshly grated Parmesan cheese (see page 22)

½ cup whole milk

½ teaspoon freshly cracked black pepper

Add-ins, as desired (see below)

Add-In Suggestions

MEDITERRANEAN
- Pitted olives
- Crumbled feta cheese
- Toasted pine nuts
- Artichoke hearts, drained and roughly chopped

CHILDHOOD THROWBACK
- Frozen peas, thawed
- Tuna or other tinned fish, optional
- Toasted breadcrumbs

TUSCAN
- White beans, drained and rinsed
- Sun-dried tomatoes
- Fresh flat-leaf parsley leaves

1. Fill a large pot with 4 quarts water and add 2 teaspoons of the salt. Bring to a boil over high heat. Add the pasta and cook until al dente according to package instructions.

2. Meanwhile, in a large skillet, melt the butter over medium-high heat. Once the butter is sizzling, add the cheese, milk, pepper, and the remaining ¼ teaspoon salt. Whisk until combined, then remove the skillet from the heat.

3. Drain the pasta, then immediately add it to the sauce and toss to coat. Stir in whatever fixings you have in your pantry and serve.

BLACK BEAN TOSTADAS WITH AVOCADO-CORN SALAD

Serves 4 to 6
Prep Time: 5 Minutes
Cook Time: 25 Minutes
<35 Minutes
Dairy-Free
Kid-Friendly
Vegetarian

Ah, the tostada. What's not to love? It's like the nacho bite of your dreams. The key to making great ones at home is a freshly fried shell. While we're major no-shamers when it comes to store-bought ingredients, tostada shells from the market just don't cut it. They're a bit too dry, and of course, they're not warm. But all you need to do to get that crunchy, chewy texture is give some tortillas a quick fry. We promise it's simple, fast, and 100 percent worth it. After that, these tostadas basically make themselves, with seasoned beans and a queso-flecked corn salad. While we love fresh corn, sometimes frozen is a better way to go, like, say, when it's not corn season. Preserved at the peak of ripeness, corn is one of the many veggies that take beautifully to freezing. You don't even have to thaw it first.

1. In the base of a blender or food processor, combine the black beans and taco seasoning. Add ⅔ cup water and pulse until the beans are broken down into a thick paste, 1 to 2 minutes.

2. Transfer the beans to a small saucepan over medium-low heat. Cook, stirring often, until warmed through, about 5 minutes. Reduce the heat to low to keep warm.

3. Heat the vegetable oil in a medium skillet over medium heat. Once the oil glistens, add one tortilla and cook until golden and crisp, 1 to 2 minutes per side. Set aside on a paper towel–lined plate. Repeat with the remaining tortillas, adding more oil to the skillet as needed.

4. Drain off all but 1 teaspoon of the oil from the skillet. Add the corn and cook, stirring occasionally, until warmed through, about 3 minutes. Transfer the corn to a medium bowl and add the arugula, queso fresco (if desired), cilantro, avocado, lime juice, and salt. Stir to combine.

5. Divide the beans evenly among the toasted tortillas, spreading them into a thin layer. Spoon the avocado-corn salad over the top and serve with the pickled onions.

1 (15.5-ounce) can black beans, drained and rinsed

1 tablespoon Taco Seasoning (page 267)

¼ cup vegetable oil, plus more as needed

6 (6-inch) corn tortillas

1 cup fresh or frozen corn kernels

2 cups loosely packed arugula

½ cup crumbled queso fresco (optional)

¼ cup loosely packed chopped fresh cilantro

1 avocado, diced

2 teaspoons fresh lime juice (from 1 lime)

¼ teaspoon kosher salt

⅓ cup Pickled Onions, drained (page 268)

Serves 4
Prep Time: 20 Minutes
Cook Time: 50 Minutes
Dairy-Free
Gluten-Free
Vegetarian

CRISPY SMASHED POTATOES WITH GRIBICHE

Made with hard-boiled eggs instead of raw, sauce gribiche exists in a world of its own, somewhere adjacent to tartar sauce and rémoulade. Recipes vary a bit here and there, but they always include hard-boiled eggs and often call for capers or cornichons. Our version gets its briny quality from Castelvetrano olives, which, along with flat-leaf parsley, pull this classic French sauce over into Italy. A textural, flavorful, colorful condiment, gribiche goes well with many things, but we think it lives its best life served over a plate of salty, crispy smashed potatoes.

6 tablespoons extra-virgin olive oil, plus more for greasing

Fine sea salt

1 pound new potatoes

3 Persian cucumbers, cut into 1-inch pieces

2 tablespoons distilled white vinegar

1 tablespoon stone-ground mustard

4 hard-boiled eggs, roughly chopped

¼ cup roughly chopped pitted Castelvetrano olives

2 tablespoons chopped fresh flat-leaf parsley leaves

½ pound asparagus, ends trimmed, cut into 2-inch pieces

Freshly cracked black pepper

1. Preheat the oven to 475°F with a rack in the center position. Grease a rimmed sheet pan with olive oil.

2. Add a generous pinch of salt to a large pot of water and bring to a boil over high heat. Add the potatoes and cook until just tender, 15 to 20 minutes. Strain the potatoes in a colander and let cool for about 5 minutes.

3. Meanwhile, make the gribiche. Using the side of a knife, smash the cucumber pieces until they're roughly broken. In a medium bowl, stir together 3 tablespoons of the olive oil, the vinegar, mustard, and 1 teaspoon of salt. Add the smashed cucumbers, the eggs, olives, and parsley and toss to combine.

4. Spread out the potatoes on the prepared sheet pan. Using the bottom of a drinking glass, smash the potatoes until each is about ¼ inch thick. Drizzle the remaining 3 tablespoons oil all over the potatoes and sprinkle them with 1 teaspoon salt.

5. Bake the potatoes for 15 minutes, then add the asparagus to the sheet pan (overlapping is okay) and bake for about 10 more minutes, or until the potatoes are crispy and the asparagus is tender.

6. To serve, transfer the potatoes and asparagus to a serving platter. Top evenly with the gribiche and freshly cracked black pepper.

HERB SALAD
WITH FRIED FETA

Serves 2
Prep Time: 15 Minutes
Cook Time: 5 Minutes
<35 Minutes
Vegetarian

That's right—this salad calls for two whole cups of parsley. It's not a typo! You know how annoying it is when you only need a tiny bit of parsley to garnish a dish and end up with the rest of the bunch wilting away in your fridge? Now you know exactly what to do with it! Fresh and good for you, it can absolutely stand on its own, and we think it's about time to let it. Here, we use this power herb as a foil for warm, salty fried feta and a minty lemon dressing. If you've never pan-fried cheese before, welcome to a world of deliciousness. Feta is sturdy enough to hold up to the heat; it doesn't melt, instead holding its shape while softening and yielding a gorgeous crust.

1. In a large bowl, toss together the parsley, tomatoes, red onion, mint, garlic, the 2 tablespoons olive oil, the lemon juice, kosher salt, and pepper.

2. In a shallow bowl, beat the egg. In a separate shallow bowl, place the panko. Working with one piece of feta at a time, dip the feta in the egg, turning to coat and allowing the excess to drip off. Then set the feta in the panko, pressing to adhere. (See Note on dredging, page 203.)

3. Heat the ⅓ cup oil in a small skillet over medium heat. Once the oil is glistening, add the feta and cook, undisturbed, until golden brown on the bottom, 1 to 2 minutes. Flip and repeat on the other side, 1 to 2 more minutes.

4. Divide the herb salad between 2 plates and top each with the fried feta. Season to taste with flaky salt (if desired) and more pepper.

2 cups packed fresh flat-leaf parsley leaves

1 pint cherry tomatoes, halved

½ small red onion, thinly sliced (about ¼ cup)

2 tablespoons fresh mint leaves, roughly chopped

2 garlic cloves, minced

⅓ cup plus 2 tablespoons extra-virgin olive oil

¼ cup fresh lemon juice (from 2 lemons)

¼ teaspoon kosher salt

¼ teaspoon freshly cracked black pepper, plus more for serving

1 large egg

½ cup panko breadcrumbs

1 (7-ounce) block feta cheese, halved

Flaky salt, for serving (optional)

Serves 4
Prep Time: 10 Minutes
Cook Time: 30 Minutes
Dairy-Free
Gluten-Free
Vegetarian

HUMMUS BOWL WITH ROASTED CAULIFLOWER

A whole cupboard full of spices—za'atar, cayenne, smoked paprika, and cumin—enliven crispy baked chickpeas, and those crisp, protein-packed baubles in turn bring texture and excitement to a bowl built from hummus and simple roasted cauliflower. Filling, healthy, textural, and just a little bit spicy, this hearty bowl is a keeper.

1 tablespoon za'atar, plus more for serving (see Note on page 121)

1 teaspoon ground cumin

1 teaspoon kosher salt

½ teaspoon smoked paprika

½ teaspoon cayenne pepper

4 cups cauliflower florets (from 1 large head)

1 (15.5-ounce) can chickpeas, drained and rinsed

¼ cup extra-virgin olive oil, plus more for serving

2 cups classic hummus

1 cup loosely packed arugula or microgreens

1 large carrot, peeled and ribboned (see Note)

4 tablespoons finely chopped fresh mint

1. Preheat the oven to 400°F with a rack in the center position.

2. In a small bowl, mix together the za'atar, cumin, salt, paprika, and cayenne. On a rimmed sheet pan, combine the cauliflower, chickpeas, and olive oil. Toss to coat well. Sprinkle on the spice mixture, toss to coat, and spread the cauliflower and chickpeas into a single layer. Bake for 30 minutes, or until the cauliflower is golden brown and the chickpeas are crispy. Remove from the oven and let cool slightly.

3. Smear the hummus onto the bottoms of 4 bowls, dividing evenly. Add the roasted cauliflower and chickpeas. Scatter the arugula, carrot, and mint over the top. Drizzle each bowl with more olive oil and sprinkle with a pinch of za'atar.

Note: Ribboning a carrot is easy—just run a vegetable peeler straight down its length.

PAN-FRIED POLENTA WITH BLISTERED TOMATOES AND BURRATA

Serves 4
Prep Time: 5 Minutes
Cook Time: 40 Minutes
Gluten-Free
Vegetarian

When the tomatoes are about ready to jump off the vine and fresh basil is abundant and so fragrant—isn't it nice how those things always happen at the same time?—you have to make this sun-soaked recipe. It's finger food-y enough to work as an appetizer, but the milky, cream-filled burrata and pan-fried polenta offer plenty of heft, so don't overlook its strength as a summertime main dish. It's best served with a chilled glass of wine and a soft August breeze.

1. Line a rimmed quarter sheet pan (9 x 13 inches; see Note) with parchment paper, leaving a bit of overhang on either short side.

2. Fill a medium pot with 4 cups water and add 1 teaspoon of the fine salt. Bring to a boil over high heat. Reduce the heat to medium-low and slowly whisk in the polenta. Cook, whisking often, until the polenta is softened, about 15 minutes. Stir in the butter to melt, then remove the pot from the heat. Spread the polenta onto the prepared sheet pan and use the back of a spoon to smooth out the top. Let cool completely, about 15 minutes.

3. Meanwhile, heat 2 tablespoons of the olive oil in a large skillet over medium-high heat. Once the oil is glistening, add the cherry tomatoes. Cook, undisturbed, until the tomatoes start to blister, about 10 minutes. Add the garlic, thyme, and the remaining ½ teaspoon fine salt and cook until fragrant, about 2 more minutes. Transfer to a medium bowl.

4. Carefully remove the polenta from the pan, lifting it by the parchment overhang, and transfer to a cutting board. Cut the polenta into 9 even pieces, each about 3 x 4 inches.

5. Wipe out the skillet from the tomatoes and add the remaining 2 tablespoons olive oil over medium-high heat. Once the oil is glistening, working in batches, add the polenta and cook until golden brown, 4 to 5 minutes per side. Transfer to a serving platter.

6. Spoon the tomato mixture over each piece of fried polenta. Tear the burrata over the top, dividing evenly. Spoon over any excess oil from the tomatoes. Top with fresh basil, pepper, and flaky salt and serve.

1½ teaspoons fine sea salt

1 cup polenta

4 tablespoons (½ stick) unsalted butter

4 tablespoons extra-virgin olive oil

1 pint cherry tomatoes

6 garlic cloves, thinly sliced

1 tablespoon fresh thyme leaves

8 ounces burrata, drained

6 fresh basil leaves, thinly sliced

Freshly cracked black pepper

Flaky salt

Note: If you don't own a quarter sheet pan, a 9 x 13-inch baking dish will work just fine.

Serves: 4

Prep Time: 5 Minutes

Cook Time: 1 Hour to 1 Hour 15 Minutes

Dairy-Free

Gluten-Free

Kid-Friendly

EVERYDAY ROAST CHICKEN

Dinner doesn't get much more classic than roast chicken, and making one is really quite simple, so don't let it intimidate you. Just two ingredients—a chicken and some salt—yield a beautifully baked bird with crisp skin and juicy meat for an always-impressive, everyday feast. Our best tip for success is to buy the best quality bird you can find, but never one that exceeds five pounds! The larger the bird, the more difficult it will be to cook evenly. The only other thing you need to know is that kosher salt is the only salt for this job—nothing else will do. As for how to eat your perfectly golden brown, moist, Rockwell-esque roast chicken? It can be used in or on just about anything, but our favorite way to enjoy it is straight from the skillet, with a spread of a few sauces for dipping and a green salad alongside.

1 (3½- to 5-pound) chicken

2 tablespoons kosher salt

FOR SERVING (OPTIONAL)

Basil Pesto (page 267)

Buttermilk Ranch Dressing (page 274)

Chimichurri (page 271)

Green Goddess Dressing (page 272)

Romesco Sauce (page 275)

1. Preheat the oven to 375°F with a rack in the center position.

2. Pat the chicken completely dry inside and out. Set the chicken, breast side up, in a large ovenproof skillet or roasting dish. If desired, tie the legs together with kitchen string and tuck the wing tips under the body of the chicken.

3. Season the chicken all over, inside and out, with the salt.

4. Roast the chicken for 15 minutes per pound. Begin checking for doneness when 20 minutes remain (see Note).

5. Allow the chicken to rest for 15 minutes. Carve and serve with your desired sauces alongside.

Note: As a good rule of thumb, chickens roast at 375°F for 15 minutes per pound. If your bird is bigger or smaller than what a recipe calls for, you can just do the math! A chicken is always done cooking when the internal temperature taken at the thickest part of the thigh reaches 165°F on an instant-read thermometer, and the juices run clear.

BASIL CHICKEN AND BROCCOLI STIR-FRY

Serves 4
Prep Time: 15 Minutes
Cook Time: 15 Minutes
<35 Minutes
Dairy-Free
Gluten-Free
Kid-Friendly

Fast, easy, and healthy: These are a few of our favorite things when it comes to weeknight dinners, and they all perfectly describe this stir-fry. But that definitely doesn't mean it's boring or tasteless. A quick boil ensures your chicken and broccoli will be perfectly tender, while high-heat cooking lends crispy, browned edges. This sauce is full of flavor with hits of salty, sweet, and spicy at once. The basil at the end—a whole cup of it—is the crown jewel. Trust us—you won't want to skimp on it. And while it's traditional to make a stir-fry in a wok, you don't necessarily need one. Your trusty skillet will get the job done just fine.

1. Fill a large pot with water and add 2 teaspoons of the salt. Place over high heat and bring to a boil. Add the broccoli and cook until bright green and slightly tender, about 2 minutes. Using a slotted spoon, remove the broccoli and set aside, reserving the seasoned water in the pot, boiling over high heat.

2. Season the chicken all over with the remaining 1 teaspoon salt. Add the cornstarch to a medium bowl. Add the chicken and toss to coat evenly. Add the chicken to the reserved seasoned water over high heat, return to a boil, and cook until opaque, about 4 minutes. Drain the chicken and set aside.

3. In a small bowl, combine the soy sauce, oyster sauce, sambal oelek, and garlic.

4. Heat the vegetable oil in a large skillet over medium heat. Once the oil is glistening, add the broccoli and cook, stirring occasionally, until beginning to brown, about 4 minutes. Add the chicken, cashews, and soy sauce mixture. Stir to combine. Cook until the sauce is slightly thickened, about 2 minutes.

5. Remove the skillet from the heat, stir in the basil leaves, and cook until just wilted, about 1 minute more. Divide the stir-fry among 4 plates, serving it over rice.

3 teaspoons fine sea salt

8 ounces broccoli florets (about 4 cups)

1 pound boneless, skinless chicken breasts, thinly sliced

2 tablespoons cornstarch

¼ cup low-sodium soy sauce or tamari

1 tablespoon oyster sauce

1 tablespoon sambal oelek or other chili paste

4 garlic cloves, minced

1 tablespoon vegetable oil

½ cup raw cashews

1 cup loosely packed basil leaves

Cooked rice, for serving

Serves 4 to 6
Prep Time: 25 Minutes
Cook Time: 1 Hour 15 Minutes
Kid-Friendly

FRIED CHICKEN WITH SLAW

We love fried chicken so much that, years ago, we set out to master the classic dish to match our cravings. For an entire summer, you could find us at the neighborhood pool with a bag of test-fried chicken in hand, eager to share with anyone hungry enough to try it. We love boneless, skinless thighs (though bone-in, skin-on chicken works too) so we always have the option of slapping it on a bun with slaw if and when a fried-chicken-sandwich mood strikes. You don't need a deep fryer or anything fancy like that—just a deep, heavy-bottomed pot, a frying thermometer, and a good appetite. Remove your chicken from the fridge about an hour before you get started, and we'll walk you through the rest!

SLAW

¼ cup mayonnaise

1 tablespoon unfiltered apple cider vinegar (or pickle brine; see Note)

2 teaspoons sugar

½ teaspoon kosher salt

4 cups thinly sliced red cabbage (12 ounces)

CHICKEN

2 to 3 pounds boneless, skinless chicken thighs, at room temperature

1 tablespoon plus 1½ teaspoons kosher salt

2 large eggs

2½ cups buttermilk

5 cups all-purpose flour

3 tablespoons garlic powder

2 teaspoons cayenne pepper

1 tablespoon plus ¼ teaspoon freshly cracked black pepper

3 quarts vegetable oil, for frying

Spicy pickles, for serving (optional)

Note: If you're opting in on the spicy pickles for serving, you can use the briny liquid from the jar in your slaw in place of the apple cider vinegar.

1. **Make the slaw.** In a large bowl, stir together the mayonnaise, vinegar, sugar, and salt. Add the cabbage and toss to combine. Cover and place in the refrigerator.

2. **Make the chicken.** Season the chicken all over with 1 teaspoon of the salt.

3. In a shallow bowl, beat the eggs with the buttermilk. Whisk in 1½ cups of the flour, 1 tablespoon of the garlic powder, 1 teaspoon of the cayenne pepper, ½ teaspoon of the salt, and ¼ teaspoon of the black pepper to combine. In a separate shallow bowl, stir together the remaining 3½ cups flour, 2 tablespoons garlic powder, 1 tablespoon each salt and black pepper, and 1 teaspoon cayenne. (See Note on dredging, page 203.) Add the chicken to the buttermilk mixture and toss to coat well.

4. Set a cooling rack inside a rimmed sheet pan.

5. Attach a deep-fry thermometer to the side of a large, heavy pot. Add the vegetable oil to the pot over medium-high heat. Once the oil reaches 325°F, working with one piece at a time, begin removing the chicken from the wet mixture, allowing any excess to drip off. Roll it through the dry mixture, pressing to adhere. Carefully add the chicken to the hot oil, 2 to 3 pieces at a time, and cook, turning halfway through, until deep golden brown and the internal temperature of the chicken reaches 165°F on an instant-read thermometer, 10 to 12 minutes. Transfer the chicken to the cooling rack to cool. Repeat with the remaining chicken, allowing the oil to return to 325°F between batches.

6. Arrange the fried chicken on a platter. Serve with spicy pickles (if desired) and the slaw.

Serves 6
Prep Time: 10 Minutes
Cook Time: 1 Hour 15 Minutes
Gluten-Free
Kid-Friendly

ROAST CHICKEN WITH MUSHROOM CREAM SAUCE

A whole roast chicken is inherently simple and always elegant. It can be a satisfying centerpiece for a dinner party, or a quiet, classic Sunday night workhorse supper for one or two that you can eat off of all week long. Here, we utilize the roast chicken drippings, which are often overlooked but full of flavor. They provide a base for a uniquely umami-rich mushroom cream sauce that comes together quickly after roasting and knocks this particular recipe out of the stratosphere. Patting the chicken dry will ensure a crispy skin, too. It's guaranteed to impress whoever you're feeding, even if that person is just yourself.

1 (3½- to 5-pound) chicken

1 tablespoon kosher salt

1 pound cremini mushrooms, quartered

2 tablespoons unsalted butter

1 cup heavy cream

2 tablespoons low-sodium soy sauce or tamari

1 tablespoon fresh thyme leaves

Note: Patting the chicken dry will ensure a crispy skin.

1. Preheat the oven to 375°F with a rack in the center position.

2. Pat your chicken completely dry, inside and out, with paper towels. Season the chicken inside and out with the salt. Set the chicken, breast side up, in a large cast-iron skillet. If desired, tie the legs together with kitchen string and tuck the wing tips under the body.

3. Roast the chicken for 15 minutes per pound. When about 20 minutes remain, begin to check for doneness. The chicken is done when the internal temperature at the thickest part of the thigh reaches 165°F on an instant-read thermometer and the juices run clear. Transfer the chicken to a serving platter to rest while you make the sauce.

4. Using a slotted spoon, skim any large pieces of skin off the bottom of the skillet and discard them. Place the skillet over medium heat. Add the mushrooms and cook, stirring occasionally, until just tender, about 5 minutes. Stir in the butter. Once the butter begins to bubble, add the cream, soy sauce, and thyme. Reduce the heat to a low simmer and cook, stirring often, until the sauce is thickened slightly, 6 to 7 minutes.

5. Carve the chicken and top with the mushroom sauce. Serve family-style.

STUFFED CHICKEN BREAST WITH MOZZARELLA AND CREAMY KALE

Serves 4
Prep Time: 15 Minutes
Cook Time: 40 Minutes
Gluten-Free
Kid-Friendly

For Natalie, Sunday dinner with the whole extended family is a tradition. While it doesn't necessarily mean an hours-long cooking fest, it does always mean comfort food. (She once suggested salmon and salad and was quickly shut down with "save that for a Monday.") Sundays call for the kind of warm, food coma–inducing recipes that soothe and satisfy. Overflowing with cheesy, creamy, garlic-scented kale stuffing, these chicken breasts are exactly that. Homey and unfussy, they're what we all want to gather around at the end of the weekend.

1. Preheat the oven to 375°F.

2. Place the chicken on a cutting board. Using a small knife, carefully cut a 3-inch slit into the side of each chicken breast, wiggling the knife back and forth to create as much of a pocket as possible without cutting all the way through the chicken. Season the chicken inside and out with the salt.

3. Heat 2 tablespoons of the olive oil in a large ovenproof skillet over medium heat. Once the oil is glistening, add the kale and cook, stirring, until beginning to wilt, about 5 minutes. Add the garlic and cook until fragrant, about 1 more minute. Transfer the kale mixture to a medium bowl. Add the cream cheese, mozzarella, and basil and stir to combine. Carefully stuff the filling into the pockets of the chicken breasts, dividing evenly.

4. Add the remaining 1 tablespoon oil to the same skillet over medium heat. Once the oil is glistening, add the chicken and sear until golden brown, 3 to 4 minutes per side. Transfer the skillet to the oven and bake for 18 to 20 minutes, until the internal temperature of the chicken reaches 165°F on an instant-read thermometer.

5. Divide the chicken among 4 plates and spoon any juices from the skillet over the top. Serve.

4 boneless, skinless chicken breasts (about 2½ pounds total)

2 teaspoons kosher salt

3 tablespoons extra-virgin olive oil

4 cups stemmed and roughly chopped curly kale

4 garlic cloves, minced

4 ounces cream cheese, softened

4 ounces shredded mozzarella cheese

10 fresh basil leaves, roughly chopped

Serves 6
Prep Time: 15 Minutes
Cook Time: 1 Hour 15 Minutes
Gluten-Free

CHICKEN IN WINE

Coq au vin. Sounds fancy, right? Here's the thing—just because something has a French name and is cooked in a lot of wine doesn't mean you need a culinary degree to pull it off. This dish is our riff on the classic French stew, so we're just calling it like it is—chicken in wine—and it's every bit as simple as it sounds. In fact, we believe this inherently humble meal tastes best when it finds its way to our table on a random Wednesday night. Why? Because rather than being served as part of a "special occasion," the succulent, wine-braised, butter-finished chicken is an occasion in its own right.

4 pounds bone-in, skin-on chicken drumsticks and thighs

1 tablespoon kosher salt

1 teaspoon freshly cracked black pepper

2 tablespoons extra-virgin olive oil

4 small shallots, quartered

8 ounces cremini mushrooms, halved

6 garlic cloves, minced

1 (750-milliliter) bottle dry white wine, such as sauvignon blanc

2 large carrots, peeled and cut into 2-inch pieces

2 sprigs fresh thyme

3 tablespoons salted butter, cold

Chopped fresh flat-leaf parsley leaves, for serving

1. Pat the chicken dry. Season all over with the salt and pepper.

2. Heat the olive oil in a Dutch oven or braiser over medium-high heat. Once the oil is glistening, working in batches as needed, add the chicken, skin side down, and cook, undisturbed, until the skin begins to brown, about 6 minutes. Flip the chicken and repeat on the other side. Transfer the chicken to a plate.

3. To the same pan over medium heat, add the shallots and mushrooms. Cook, stirring occasionally, until softened, about 3 minutes. Add the garlic and cook until fragrant, about 1 more minute. Pour in the wine and scrape up any browned bits from the bottom of the pan. Increase the heat to high and bring to a boil, then reduce to a simmer and cook until the wine is reduced by half, about 10 minutes.

4. Add the chicken, carrots, and thyme. Increase the heat to high and return to a boil, then reduce the heat to low. Cover and cook until the internal temperature of the chicken reaches 165°F on an instant-read thermometer, about 30 minutes. Transfer the chicken to a plate.

5. Return the sauce to a simmer and cook until reduced by half, about 10 minutes. One tablespoon at a time, slowly stir in the cold butter, letting each addition melt completely before adding the next. Pick out the thyme stems, reserving the leaves in the pan, and discard.

6. Return the chicken to the pan and turn to coat in the sauce. Top with parsley and serve family-style.

COCONUT RICE BOWL WITH CILANTRO LIME CHICKEN

Serves 8
Prep Time: 20 Minutes
Cook Time: 40 Minutes
Dairy-Free
Gluten-Free
Kid-Friendly

A quick marinade of lime, garlic, cilantro, and a touch of honey transforms boneless, skinless chicken thighs into the juicy, tender surge of sunshine your dinner routine needs. Obviously we love this marinade for chicken thighs, but it might be one you'll want to memorize and use on just about everything. Try rubbing it on a whole chicken for a savory-citrusy roasted bird, slathering it on a meaty white fish like halibut before throwing it on the grill, or tossing it with fresh fruit and veggies, like we've done here. Serve this over rich coconut rice—easier to make than you think—and you'll be feeling those warm, tropical vibes for days, whatever the weather.

1. In a medium bowl, whisk together the olive oil, lime zest, the ½ cup lime juice, the cilantro, honey, chili powder, salt, and pepper. Transfer ½ cup of the marinade to a small bowl and reserve.

2. In a large bowl or plastic zip-top bag, combine the chicken, the remaining marinade, and the garlic. Turn to coat the chicken well. Let marinate at room temperature for 15 minutes or refrigerated for up to 2 hours.

3. Heat a large nonstick skillet over medium-high heat. Working in batches, add the chicken thighs in a single layer and cook, undisturbed, until the internal temperature of the chicken reaches 165°F on an instant-read thermometer, 4 to 6 minutes per side. Transfer the chicken to a cutting board. Let rest for 10 minutes, then cut into ½-inch-thick slices. Pour ¼ cup of the reserved marinade over the chicken and toss to coat.

4. In a small bowl, combine the cucumber, mango, the remaining ¼ cup reserved marinade, and the 1 tablespoon lime juice or to taste.

5. To serve, divide the coconut rice among 6 bowls. Top with the chicken and cucumber-mango salad. Garnish with fresh cilantro.

⅔ cup extra-virgin olive oil

1 tablespoon grated lime zest

½ cup plus 1 tablespoon fresh lime juice (from 4 limes)

⅓ cup finely minced fresh cilantro, plus more for serving

2 tablespoons honey

2 tablespoons chili powder

1½ teaspoons kosher salt

½ teaspoon freshly cracked black pepper

3 pounds boneless, skinless chicken thighs

6 garlic cloves, minced

2 cups diced English or Persian cucumber

1 large mango, peeled, pitted, and cut into ½-inch dice (1½ cups)

Coconut Rice, for serving (recipe follows)

continues

Coconut Rice

MAKES 6 CUPS

1 (14-ounce) can full-fat coconut milk, shaken
1 tablespoon sugar
½ teaspoon kosher salt
2 cups long-grain white rice, rinsed (see Note)

In a medium saucepan, stir together the coconut milk, 1 cup water, the sugar, and the salt. Bring to a boil over medium-high heat. Stir in the rice and return to a boil. Reduce the heat to low, cover, and cook until the liquid has been absorbed, about 20 minutes. Remove the lid and fluff the rice using a fork. Turn off the heat and let the rice sit on the hot stove for another 2 to 3 minutes before serving.

Note: Don't skip the step of rinsing your rice. First of all, it's quick and easy—just put it in a fine-mesh sieve and run some tap water through it. But most important, rinsing the rice before you cook it washes away some of the starch from its surface. Doing so will help ensure your finished coconut rice is fluffy instead of mushy or gummy. You'll know the rice is properly rinsed when the water runs clear.

CREAMY GARLIC CHICKEN PASTA

Serves 4
Prep Time: 15 Minutes
Cook Time: 30 Minutes
Kid-Friendly

When we crave a big bowl of creamy pasta, many of us think of alfredo. We do love that buttery, rich dish, but this particular cream-enriched sauce is a bit of a departure from alfredo, and a welcome one at that. Brightened with white wine, lemon, and garlic, this pasta is a bit lighter, a bit zestier, and—we think—a lot more exciting. Any long pasta that you love will work here, but our very favorite is perfectly al dente straws of bucatini. Freshly grated Parmigiano-Reggiano cheese will yield the best results here; the pre-shredded stuff just won't melt into the sauce the way it should.

1. Fill a large pot with 4 quarts water and add 2 teaspoons of the salt. Bring to a boil over high heat. Add the bucatini and cook until al dente according to the package instructions. Drain.

2. Meanwhile, heat the olive oil in a Dutch oven or large saucepan over medium-high heat. Season the chicken with 1 teaspoon of the salt and the pepper. Once the oil is glistening, add the chicken and cook, tossing occasionally, until browned on the outside and no longer pink in the middle, 8 to 10 minutes. Using a slotted spoon, transfer the chicken to a plate.

3. To the same pan over medium-high heat, add the wine and garlic. Cook, scraping up any browned bits from the bottom, until the wine has reduced by half and the garlic is softened, about 5 minutes. Add the butter and whisk until melted. Sprinkle in the flour and cook, whisking continuously, until fully incorporated, about 2 minutes. Pour in the chicken stock, heavy cream, Parmesan, and remaining ½ teaspoon salt. Increase the heat to high and bring the liquid to a boil, then reduce the heat to medium-low and cook, stirring, until the sauce begins to thicken, about 10 minutes.

4. Remove the pan from the heat. Stir in the lemon zest and juice. Add the bucatini, chicken, and parsley and toss to coat. Serve immediately with more Parmesan and freshly cracked pepper.

3½ teaspoons kosher salt

¾ pound bucatini

2 tablespoons extra-virgin olive oil

1 pound boneless, skinless chicken breast, cut into 1-inch pieces

¼ teaspoon freshly cracked black pepper, plus more for serving

1 cup dry white wine, such as sauvignon blanc

6 garlic cloves, minced

2 tablespoons unsalted butter

3 tablespoons all-purpose flour

¾ cup chicken stock

1 cup heavy cream

½ cup freshly grated Parmesan cheese, plus more for serving

1 teaspoon grated lemon zest

1 tablespoon fresh lemon juice (from 1 lemon)

¼ cup chopped fresh flat-leaf parsley leaves

Serves 8
Prep Time: 30 Minutes
Cook Time: 40 Minutes
Dairy-Free
Gluten-Free
Kid-Friendly

SMOKY CHICKEN SKEWERS WITH CORN SALAD

Inspired by the smoky, tangy heat of harissa—a fiery North African chili paste that's often flecked with garlic, saffron, or even rose petals—this punchy marinade brings regular old chicken thighs to life with its brilliant ruby-red hue and vibrant complexity. If it's summertime, these skewers—you'll want metal or soaked bamboo ones—are definitely grill-ready, so feel free to cook them that way. But, just between us, we dreamt up this recipe in the dead of winter. Longing for brighter days, we reached for warmth the best way we know how.

1 (12-ounce) jar roasted red peppers, drained

6 whole garlic cloves plus 1 minced garlic clove

5 tablespoons extra-virgin olive oil

3 tablespoons red wine vinegar

2 tablespoons smoked paprika

3½ teaspoons kosher salt

¼ teaspoon cayenne pepper

3 pounds boneless, skinless chicken thighs, cut into 1-inch pieces

5 ears corn (or 3½ cups frozen corn, thawed; see Note)

½ cup chopped fresh cilantro

1 small shallot, finely chopped

½ teaspoon freshly cracked black pepper

½ cup mayonnaise

Note: If you can't find fresh corn, you can always thaw frozen kernels and skip the boiling and slicing steps. One ear of corn equals about ¾ cup.

1. Preheat the oven to 425°F with a rack in the center position. Line a rimmed sheet pan with foil or parchment paper and set a cooling rack inside.

2. In the base of a blender or food processor, combine the red peppers, 6 whole garlic cloves, 2 tablespoons of the olive oil, 2 tablespoons of the vinegar, the paprika, 2 teaspoons of the salt, and the cayenne. Blend until smooth, about 2 minutes. Transfer ¼ cup of the marinade to a small bowl. Transfer the remainder to a large bowl or plastic zip-top bag.

3. Add the chicken to the marinade in the large bowl and toss to coat well. Let marinate for at least 10 minutes or up to 2 hours in the refrigerator.

4. Remove the chicken from the marinade and allow any excess to drip off. Tightly thread the meat onto 8 skewers, dividing evenly. Place the skewers on the prepared rack and season the chicken with 1 teaspoon salt. Bake for 20 minutes, then turn on the broiler and cook until the edges begin to brown and the chicken is cooked through, 5 to 7 more minutes.

5. Meanwhile, bring a large pot of water to a boil. Add the corn and cook until just tender, about 3 minutes. Drain and rinse in cold water just until cool enough to handle. Slice the kernels off the cobs and place them in a large bowl. Add the cilantro, shallot, minced garlic, the remaining 3 tablespoons oil, remaining 1 tablespoon vinegar, remaining ½ teaspoon salt, and the black pepper.

6. Add the mayonnaise to the reserved marinade in the small bowl and stir to mix well.

7. Arrange the corn salad on a serving platter. Lay the chicken skewers on top. Serve family-style with the smoky mayo alongside for dipping.

Smoky Chicken Skewers with Corn Salad, *page 116*

CHICKEN STRIPS
WITH ZA'ATAR RANCH

Serves 4

Prep Time: 15 Minutes

Cook Time: 20 Minutes

<35 Minutes

Kid-Friendly

Sheet Pan

A dinner to feed your inner child, but that your sophisticated, grown-up self will love, too. How, exactly? Say hello to za'atar, the irresistible Middle Eastern spice blend with a tangy kick. Here, it lends both the homemade buttermilk ranch dip and the chicken strips themselves a major sophistication makeover. Slipping an unfamiliar flavor into a familiar food is a great way to introduce kids to something new. And let's be real—it's not like you ever outgrew your love for piping-hot, crispy-crunchy pieces of chicken. Won't it be nice to dip them in something exciting?

1. Preheat the oven to 425°F with a rack in the center position. Set a cooling rack inside a rimmed sheet pan.

2. Place the flour in a shallow bowl. In a separate shallow bowl, stir together the panko, za'atar, and garlic powder. In a third shallow bowl, beat the eggs. (See Note on dredging, page 203.)

3. Season the chicken tenders with the salt. Working with one piece at a time, dip the chicken into the flour and turn to coat. Then dip the chicken into the eggs, letting the excess drip off, then into the panko mixture, pressing to create a crust. Place on the cooling rack inside the sheet pan.

4. Mist the chicken with cooking spray. Bake for about 20 minutes, or until the chicken is cooked through and the crust is golden brown. Serve the chicken tenders warm with the za'atar ranch alongside.

1 cup all-purpose flour

2 cups panko breadcrumbs

2 tablespoons za'atar (see Note)

1 teaspoon garlic powder

2 large eggs

1½ pounds chicken tenders

2 teaspoons kosher salt

Cooking spray

Za'atar Ranch, for serving (recipe follows)

Note: If you don't have za'atar, make your own. Combine 1 teaspoon ground cumin, 1 teaspoon dried thyme, 1 teaspoon sesame seeds, and ½ teaspoon kosher salt. If you have it on hand, add 1 teaspoon ground sumac as well.

Za'atar Ranch
MAKES 1½ CUPS

½ cup buttermilk

½ cup mayonnaise

½ cup sour cream

1 tablespoon za'atar (see Note)

1 teaspoon dried parsley

1 teaspoon onion powder

1 teaspoon garlic powder

1 teaspoon dried dill

½ teaspoon kosher salt

In a small bowl, whisk together the buttermilk, mayonnaise, sour cream, za'atar, parsley, onion powder, garlic powder, dill, and salt until smooth. Store refrigerated in an airtight container for up to 2 weeks.

Serves 8
Prep Time: 10 Minutes
Cook Time: 1 Hour
Dairy-Free
Kid-Friendly

BAKED PENNE CHICKEN PUTTANESCA

With bold, briny flavors and a slow-simmered tomato base, this pasta sauce, brazenly full-bodied, could only hail from the bustling streets of Naples. We can't talk about it without mentioning that "alla puttanesca" translates to "in the style of prostitutes," which is usually taken to mean that the enticing scent of this pasta was used by the, ahem, working women of Naples to lure in customers. Like so many food origin stories, this one is just that—a story. We added our own piece of the story by layering in chicken sausage for protein and herby meatiness, and by cooking dried pasta right in the baking dish for the ultimate convenience. No matter how this dish came along, we're glad it did—and we bet you will be, too.

2 tablespoons extra-virgin olive oil, plus more for greasing

12 ounces cooked Italian chicken sausage (4 links), thinly sliced

2 tablespoons capers, drained

3 garlic cloves, minced

3 anchovy fillets

1 (24-ounce) jar marinara sauce

1 pound penne or ziti

1 (14.5-ounce) can crushed tomatoes

1 teaspoon kosher salt

½ teaspoon freshly cracked black pepper

½ cup pitted Castelvetrano olives

1¼ cups chicken stock

1 cup freshly grated Parmesan cheese, plus more for serving (optional)

Minced fresh flat-leaf parsley leaves, for serving (optional)

1 teaspoon red pepper flakes, for serving (optional)

1. Preheat the oven to 375°F. Grease a 9 x 13-inch baking dish with olive oil.

2. Heat the 2 tablespoons olive oil in a large skillet over medium-high heat. Once the oil is glistening, add the sausage and cook until lightly browned on both sides, about 5 minutes. Add the capers, garlic, and anchovies. Cook, stirring to break up the anchovies, until fragrant, about 2 minutes. Add the marinara, pasta, crushed tomatoes, salt, and pepper. Stir to combine well.

3. Transfer the pasta mixture to the prepared baking dish and spread into an even layer. Stud the pasta with the olives and pour the chicken stock over the dish, pressing as much pasta down into the liquid as possible.

4. Cover the baking dish with foil and bake for 40 to 45 minutes, until the pasta is tender. Remove the dish from the oven, discard the foil, and, if desired, sprinkle the dish with the 1 cup Parmesan. Return to the oven uncovered and bake for about 10 more minutes, until the cheese is melted and the sauce is bubbling.

5. To serve, sprinkle with parsley, red pepper flakes, and more Parmesan, if desired.

CHICKEN SHAWARMA
SALAD WITH
TAHINI DRESSING

Serves 6
Prep Time: 10 Minutes
Cook Time: 20 Minutes
<35 Minutes
Gluten-Free
Kid-Friendly
Sheet Pan

You might know shawarma by one of its other names—doner kebab or gyro. Traditionally, this Turkish or Greek meat dish is made with heavily spiced lamb, chicken, or beef. The meat is shaved from the slowly spinning vertical rotisserie on which it cooks straight into a pillowy, warm pita or flatbread. Veggies and sauces are added to pack even more punch. In our version, we honor the defining big, bold flavors and crispy-edged meat, but with the ease of a sheet pan meal that takes less than thirty minutes to cook. The chicken doesn't need to marinate in the yogurt, but if you're planning ahead, it can stay in the fridge overnight. We love this as a salad, but if you want something a little heartier, feel free to get creative and serve the dish wrapped in pita, or try it over rice with a drizzle of the tahini dressing.

1. Make the chicken. Preheat the oven to 350°F with a rack in the center position.

2. In a large bowl, stir together the yogurt, cumin, cardamom, turmeric, cinnamon, and 2 teaspoons of the salt. Add the chicken and turn to coat.

3. Spread or brush 1 tablespoon of the olive oil onto a rimmed sheet pan. Remove the chicken from the marinade and arrange it on half of the sheet pan. On the other half, arrange the onion, bell peppers, and Peppadews, if using. Drizzle the remaining 1 tablespoon olive oil over the vegetables and sprinkle them with the remaining 1 teaspoon salt. Toss to combine. Bake for 20 minutes, or until the chicken is cooked through and the onions and peppers are tender.

4. Meanwhile, make the tahini dressing. In a medium bowl, combine the tahini with ⅔ cup water, the garlic, lemon juice, olive oil, and salt. The sauce will look as though it's separating; keep whisking until smooth.

5. To serve, evenly divide the romaine lettuce among 6 plates. Top with the chicken and roasted veggies, dividing evenly. Add cucumber and tomato. Drizzle over a generous amount of tahini dressing.

CHICKEN

1 cup plain Greek yogurt

2 teaspoons ground cumin

2 teaspoons ground cardamom

2 teaspoons ground turmeric

2 teaspoons ground cinnamon

3 teaspoons kosher salt

2 pounds boneless, skinless chicken breasts, cut into 1-inch strips

2 tablespoons extra-virgin olive oil

1 small red onion, halved and cut into ½-inch-thick slices

2 large red, yellow, or orange bell peppers, cut into ½-inch-thick strips

½ cup Peppadew peppers, drained (optional)

TAHINI DRESSING

1 cup tahini

4 garlic cloves, minced

½ cup fresh lemon juice (from 3 to 4 lemons)

⅓ cup extra-virgin olive oil

½ teaspoon kosher salt

8 cups roughly chopped romaine lettuce

Diced cucumber

Sliced tomato

Serves 4 to 6
Prep Time: 20 Minutes
Cook Time: 35 Minutes
Dairy-Free
Gluten-Free
Kid-Friendly

SKILLET
MISO CHICKEN

The perfect trifecta of flavors in this marinade—miso, lemon, and honey—comes from our friend Andy. We all want dinner on the table like, yesterday, but this one is worth taking your time with: The crispy charred bits on the edges of these ultra-savory chicken thighs will have everyone singing your praises. To get them, yes, you'll actually need to cook the chicken in batches so you don't overcrowd your pan. The honey in the marinade means flipping it a few times, too, so it doesn't stick—ruining your dinner AND your pan. This recipe is also a prime example of one of our favorite two-birds-one-stone tips ever: If you're making a marinade, double the recipe and use the extra as a salad dressing. You'll never regret it.

⅓ cup yellow or white miso

½ cup plus 2 teaspoons vegetable oil

2 tablespoons fresh lemon juice (from 1 to 2 lemons)

2 tablespoons honey

1 tablespoon plus 1 teaspoon rice or unfiltered apple cider vinegar

1½ teaspoons kosher salt

½ teaspoon freshly cracked black pepper

2½ pounds boneless, skinless chicken thighs (about 8)

6 cups loosely packed arugula

1. In a large bowl, whisk together the miso, ¼ cup of the vegetable oil, the lemon juice, honey, 1 tablespoon of the vinegar, the salt, and pepper until fully combined. Transfer 2 tablespoons of the miso marinade to a small bowl and reserve.

2. Add the chicken thighs to the remaining marinade and turn to coat. Marinate the chicken for 15 minutes at room temperature or up to 2 hours covered in the refrigerator.

3. Heat 2 teaspoons of the oil in a large skillet over medium-high heat. Once the oil is glistening, working in batches, add the chicken thighs in a single layer. Cook, undisturbed, until the chicken begins to brown on the bottom, about 4 minutes. Flip the chicken and repeat on the other side, about another 4 minutes. Continue to cook, flipping the chicken every 2 to 3 minutes, until cooked through, about 8 more minutes total. The chicken is ready when the internal temperature reaches 165°F on an instant-read thermometer. Transfer to a large platter.

4. Meanwhile, make the dressing. In a large bowl, whisk together the remaining ¼ cup oil, the reserved 2 tablespoons miso marinade, and the remaining 1 teaspoon vinegar until fully combined. Add the arugula and toss to coat.

5. Serve the chicken with the arugula salad alongside.

CHICKEN WITH TOMATOES IN SPICED COCONUT SIMMER SAUCE

Serves 4
Prep Time: 15 Minutes
Cook Time: 1 Hour
Dairy-Free
Gluten-Free
Kid-Friendly

For some of us, our first introduction to the flavors of Indian cuisine was via chicken tikka masala. While it may not be the most authentically Indian dish—it was likely created in the United Kingdom sometime in the mid-twentieth century, though its exact origins are murky—it has become a favorite pretty much everywhere, and for good reason. A luscious tomato sauce, enriched with coconut milk (or sometimes cream or yogurt), bountiful spices, and plenty of onion and garlic, makes a heavenly bath for chicken. In this dish, inspired by all that deliciousness, you'll simmer the chicken uncovered so its skin stays somewhat crisp while the sauce thickens up. Speaking of chicken, we're calling for leg quarters—the thigh and attached drumstick—because not only do they have lots of flavorful dark meat, but they also make for a dramatic presentation that invites everyone at your table to serve themselves generously and eat heartily.

1. Pat the chicken dry with a paper towel. Season all over with 1 teaspoon of the salt.

2. Heat the coconut or vegetable oil in a large braiser or skillet over medium heat. Once the oil is glistening, working in batches as needed, add the chicken and cook, undisturbed, until the skin is golden and crispy, 6 to 8 minutes per side. Transfer the chicken to a plate.

3. Add the onion to the same pot over medium heat and cook, stirring occasionally, until beginning to soften, about 4 minutes. Add the garlic and cook until fragrant, about 1 minute. Add the cumin, the remaining 1 teaspoon salt, the ginger, turmeric, cinnamon, cayenne, and allspice and cook, stirring, until the spices are fragrant, about 1 more minute.

4. Stir in the coconut milk and tomatoes. Increase the heat to high and bring to a simmer. Return the chicken and any collected juices to the pot, reduce the heat to medium-low, and cook until the internal temperature of the chicken reaches 165°F on an instant-read thermometer, about 30 minutes.

5. To serve, divide the chicken among 4 bowls and spoon the sauce over the top. Add a scoop of rice and/or serve with naan. Garnish with fresh cilantro, if desired.

2 to 3 pounds chicken leg quarters (thigh and attached drumstick)

2 teaspoons kosher salt

1 tablespoon coconut oil or vegetable oil

1 small yellow onion, diced

3 large garlic cloves, minced

1 tablespoon ground cumin

1 teaspoon ground ginger

1 teaspoon ground turmeric

½ teaspoon ground cinnamon

½ teaspoon cayenne pepper

¼ teaspoon ground allspice

1 (14-ounce) can full-fat coconut milk, shaken

1 (14-ounce) can crushed tomatoes

Cooked rice and/or naan, for serving

Fresh cilantro, for garnish (optional)

Serves 4
Prep Time: 5 Minutes
Cook Time: 35 Minutes
Gluten-Free

CHICKEN AND CABBAGE IN CREAM

Heavy cream in all its glory slowly softens crunchy cabbage wedges and gently cooks the chicken to perfection in a pan that's worth its weight in gold for being as functional on the stovetop as it is gorgeous on the table. If you haven't invested in a braiser or Dutch oven yet, this recipe is as good an excuse as any! Garlic and good mustard swirl in the braising liquid, giving it a French-countryside vibe that's cozy and inviting. Don't worry—your cream won't curdle as long as you keep the simmer gentle. And as for any sauce left in the pan, sop it up with some crusty bread, or if you're really going for broke, spoon it over a mountain of mashed potatoes.

3 tablespoons extra-virgin olive oil

4 boneless, skinless chicken breasts (2 to 2½ pounds)

1 teaspoon kosher salt

½ teaspoon freshly cracked black pepper

½ small cabbage, core intact, cut into 4 (2-inch-thick) wedges

1 pint cherry tomatoes

1 cup heavy cream

4 garlic cloves, roughly chopped or sliced

2 tablespoons stone-ground mustard

1 tablespoon fresh thyme leaves

1 tablespoon unfiltered apple cider vinegar

Crusty bread, mashed potatoes, cooked pasta, or rice pilaf, for serving

1. Heat 2 tablespoons of the olive oil in a large braiser or Dutch oven over medium-high heat. Season the chicken all over with the salt and pepper. Once the oil is glistening, working in batches as needed, add the chicken and cook, undisturbed, until browned, 5 to 7 minutes per side. Transfer the chicken to a plate.

2. Add the remaining 1 tablespoon oil to the braiser over medium-high heat. Add the cabbage wedges cut side down and cook, undisturbed, until browned on the bottom, 3 to 5 minutes. Flip the cabbage, add the tomatoes, and cook until the cabbage is browned on the other side, another 3 to 5 minutes.

3. Add the cream, garlic, mustard, thyme, and vinegar, scraping up any browned bits from the bottom of the pan and stirring to combine. Bring to a simmer and return the chicken to the pan. Reduce the heat to medium-low, cover, and cook until the internal temperature of the chicken reaches 165°F on an instant-read thermometer, about 15 minutes. Adjust the seasoning to taste.

4. Serve family-style with crusty bread, mashed potatoes, pasta of your choice, or rice pilaf.

NOT-SO-BASIC
CHICKEN FAJITAS

Serves 6
Prep Time: 10 Minutes
Cook Time: 25 Minutes
<35 Minutes
Dairy-Free
Gluten-Free
Kid-Friendly
Sheet Pan

Juicy, lime-spritzed chicken breast and tender veggies seasoned to perfection, fajitas might just be the ultimate please-everyone dinner. Not only are they tasty, but they're also fun to eat, as everyone gets to DIY their own with lots of topping choices. We used to make this dish by marinating the chicken for a long time and then sautéing it in a pan with the veggies, working diligently in small batches to get a perfect sear on all of it. Then we realized that if we spread it all onto a sheet pan and threw it into a hot oven, we'd have a dish that was faster, easier, and every bit as delicious!

1. Preheat the oven to 375°F with a rack in the center position.

2. In a large bowl, stir together the taco seasoning, lime juice, and olive oil. Add the chicken, bell peppers, and onion and toss to coat. Spread the mixture onto a rimmed sheet pan.

3. Bake for 15 to 20 minutes, or until the chicken is cooked through. If desired, turn the oven to broil and cook for 3 more minutes, or until the chicken is lightly charred.

4. Transfer the chicken and veggies to a serving dish. Serve with warm tortillas, salsa, avocado, sour cream, fresh cilantro, and lime wedges alongside.

¼ cup Taco Seasoning (page 267)

2 tablespoons fresh lime juice (from 1 to 2 limes)

1 tablespoon extra-virgin olive oil

2 pounds boneless, skinless chicken breast, cut against the grain into ½-inch-thick slices

1 red bell pepper, thinly sliced

1 yellow bell pepper, thinly sliced

1 green bell pepper, thinly sliced

1 small red onion, halved and thinly sliced

FOR SERVING (OPTIONAL)
12 (6-inch) tortillas, warmed

Salsa or hot sauce

Sliced avocado

Sour cream

Fresh cilantro leaves

Lime wedges

Serves 6
Prep Time: 20 Minutes
Cook Time: 1 Hour 15 Minutes
Dairy-Free
Gluten-Free

CARAWAY ROAST CHICKEN OVER CABBAGE

Caraway, dill, paprika, cabbage—we challenge you to find a more classically Eastern European quartet of ingredients. While it may not have a permanent spot on your spice rack just yet (keyword: *yet*!), we bet you've had caraway before. You'll often see these seeds lending unique, slightly citrus-liquorice-esque flavor to sauerkraut. Dill is often in the mix, too. Sweet Hungarian paprika and chicken are a pairing for the ages—we love the spice's aromatic sharpness and crimson hue. Without any help at all from you, perfectly seasoned chicken drippings will braise the cabbage as your dinner cooks. And don't forget to splurge for a good-quality grainy mustard to serve on the side. Put it all together and you get a roast chicken that'll either take you right back to Grandma's house in the old country, or make you wish you'd had a childhood filled with food memories as delicious as this.

1 (2-pound) head green cabbage, cored and cut into 1-inch wedges

3 tablespoons kosher salt

1 tablespoon caraway seeds

1 tablespoon dried dill

2 teaspoons paprika

1 (4- to 5-pound) chicken, spatchcocked (see below)

2 tablespoons extra-virgin olive oil

Grainy mustard, for serving

How to Spatchcock a Chicken

Pat the chicken dry with paper towels. Place on a large cutting board, breast side down with the neck facing toward you.

Using good-quality kitchen shears, hold the neck and cut along one side of the spine, separating it from the ribs. Be sure to cut as close to the spine as possible. Repeat on the other side of the spine. If you are having difficulty, rotate the bird so the tail faces you and cut from the other side.

Flip the chicken breast-side up. Using the palms of your hands, press along the breastbone; you might hear a crack. This should flatten the chicken completely.

1. Preheat the oven to 375°F with a rack in the center position.

2. Arrange the cabbage wedges, overlapping slightly, in a 12-inch cast-iron skillet and sprinkle with 1 teaspoon of the salt.

3. In a small bowl, stir together the remaining 2 tablespoons plus 2 teaspoons salt, the caraway, dill, and paprika.

4. Lay the chicken over the cabbage and drizzle the olive oil over the entire dish. Rub the chicken with the spice mixture, completely coating its skin.

5. Roast the chicken for about 1 hour 15 minutes, or until its internal temperature at the thickest part of the thigh reaches 165°F on an instant-read thermometer. Remove and let rest for 10 minutes.

6. Carve the chicken, then transfer it to a serving platter along with the cabbage. Serve family-style with the mustard alongside.

CHICKEN MARBELLA

Serves 6
Prep Time: 20 Minutes
Cook Time: 40 Minutes
Gluten-Free
Sheet Pan

Oh hey, 1982 is calling. It wants its favorite chicken recipe back . . . to which we respond with a resounding NOPE. Chicken Marbella is far too good to leave behind in the eighties—we loved eating it when we were young, and we love eating it now, too. Well, with a few small updates from its original appearance in *The Silver Palate Cookbook*. Here we've used our favorite time-and-effort saver, the trusty sheet pan, and we've done away with the traditional overnight marinade. To save even more time, you can make the olive paste up to twenty-four hours in advance; just transfer it to a bowl and store in the fridge. We love this meal so much, and we wanted it to be an option even on a weeknight. We promise we didn't mess with the flavors, though—we wouldn't dare.

1. Preheat the oven to 400°F with a rack in the center position.

2. **Make the olive paste.** Combine the olives, prunes, olive oil, wine, garlic, capers, oregano, salt, and pepper in a food processor. Pulse until a coarse paste forms, about 30 seconds.

3. **Make the chicken.** Arrange the chicken on a rimmed sheet pan and coat each piece with the olive paste, fully covering on all sides. Pour the chicken stock and white wine onto the sheet pan around the chicken. Drop the olives, prunes, and capers into the liquid. Sprinkle the chicken with the brown sugar and salt.

4. Bake for 30 minutes, or until the internal temperature of the chicken reaches 165°F on an instant-read thermometer. With a slotted spoon, transfer the chicken, olives, capers, and prunes to a serving platter. Sprinkle the parsley over the top.

5. Place a small saucepan over medium-high heat. Carefully pour the sheet pan drippings and solids into the saucepan. Bring the sauce to a boil, then reduce the heat to low and simmer until the liquid is reduced by half, about 5 minutes. Whisk in the butter until fully incorporated. Transfer to a small serving bowl.

6. Serve the chicken family-style with the sauce alongside.

OLIVE PASTE

⅓ cup pitted Castelvetrano olives

⅓ cup pitted prunes

¼ cup extra-virgin olive oil

¼ cup dry white wine, such as sauvignon blanc

4 garlic cloves

2 tablespoons capers, drained

1 tablespoon dried oregano

½ teaspoon kosher salt

½ teaspoon freshly cracked black pepper

CHICKEN

3 to 4 pounds bone-in, skin-on chicken drumsticks and thighs

1 cup chicken stock

⅓ cup dry white wine, such as sauvignon blanc

⅓ cup pitted Castelvetrano olives, halved

⅓ cup pitted prunes, roughly chopped

1 tablespoon capers, drained

1 tablespoon light brown sugar

1 teaspoon kosher salt

2 tablespoons finely chopped fresh flat-leaf parsley leaves

2 tablespoons unsalted butter

Serves 4
Prep Time: 15 Minutes
Cook Time: 20 Minutes
<35 Minutes
Gluten-Free

STEAK

1 tablespoon extra-virgin olive oil

1 (2-pound) rib eye steak (1½ inches thick), at room temperature

2 teaspoons kosher salt

1 teaspoon freshly cracked black pepper

2 tablespoons Herb Butter (page 276) or salted butter

SALAD

1 bunch green onions, white and green parts, thinly sliced

2 garlic cloves, thinly sliced

4 cups stemmed and roughly chopped hearty greens, such as kale or Swiss chard

1 tablespoon extra-virgin olive oil

¼ teaspoon red pepper flakes

4 cups cooked grains of choice, such as barley, farro, or brown rice, at room temperature

¼ pound radishes, thinly sliced

VINAIGRETTE

4 tablespoons Herb Butter (page 276) or salted butter, melted

2 tablespoons fresh lemon juice (from 1 lemon)

1 teaspoon Dijon mustard

1 teaspoon honey

½ teaspoon kosher salt

¼ teaspoon freshly cracked black pepper

Note: The most precise way to measure the doneness of meat is with an instant-read thermometer (see page 29). Time and temperatures are changeable, but a measurement is a measurement. For beef, rare is 125°F; medium-rare is 135°F; medium is 145°F; medium-well is 150°F; and well is 160°F. Medium-rare is our preference, but feel free to cook your steak however you like it best!

STEAK AND GRAINS WITH HERB BUTTER VINAIGRETTE

A great steak—and a rib eye is a great steak—deserves the royal treatment. But that doesn't mean you can't think outside the "steakhouse dinner plate" box. While this recipe pairs that beautifully marbled cut of beef with plenty of butter, all that indulgence is lifted by the fresh herbs, green onions, and rosy radishes. Both whisking the homemade herb butter into the vinaigrette and brushing it on the steak really ties this whole dish together.

1. **Make the steak.** Heat the olive oil in a large cast-iron skillet over high heat. Season the steak all over with the salt and pepper. Once the oil is just smoking, add the steak and cook for 6 to 8 minutes per side for medium-rare (see Note).

2. Transfer the steak to a cutting board and top with the butter. Let the steak rest for 5 to 10 minutes.

3. **Meanwhile, make the salad.** In the same skillet over medium heat, add the green onions. Cook, stirring often, until charred, about 3 minutes. Add the garlic and cook until fragrant, about 1 minute. Add the greens, olive oil, and red pepper flakes. Cook, tossing to coat, until the greens are just wilted, about 3 minutes. Transfer to a large bowl.

4. **Make the vinaigrette.** In a small bowl, whisk together the melted butter, lemon juice, mustard, honey, salt, and pepper to combine.

5. Pour the vinaigrette over the greens mixture. Add the grains and radishes and toss to combine. Slice the steak against the grain (see Note, page 173). Serve alongside the grain salad.

SKILLET PEPPERONI PIZZA WITH BLISTERED TOMATOES

Serves 4

Prep Time: 3 Hours, including rise time

Cook Time: 40 Minutes

Kid-Friendly

As longtime fans of wood-fired pizza's bubbly, thin crust, we never thought we'd have room in our hearts to love hefty pies, too. But then we fell for Detroit-style pizza—and we fell hard. While traditionally it's rectangular, we created a skillet version to bring this chewy, cheese-loaded, focaccia-like base within easy reach for making at home. When you're assembling the pizza, be sure to get the cheese cubes—yes, cubes; we didn't change *that* tradition—dotted right to the edges of the pan. As it bakes, the fat oozes out of the cheese and flows down the sides of the dough to make the crust dark, crispy, and ultra-buttery. While we call for 550°F, we know some ovens top out at 500°F, so just crank yours all the way up. We like to knead the dough by hand, but if you prefer, feel free to do it in a stand mixer fitted with the dough hook. Oh, and one last thing: If you make our homemade Buttermilk Ranch Dressing (page 274) for crust-dipping, you won't be sorry.

1. Make the crust. In a small bowl, sprinkle the yeast over the warm water. Stir briefly, then set aside to proof for 5 to 10 minutes.

2. In a large bowl, whisk together the flour and salt. Pour in the bubbly water and, using your hands, mix until a shaggy dough forms. Set aside for 10 minutes.

3. Grease a large bowl with olive oil. Turn the dough out onto a floured surface. Knead the dough with floured hands until smooth, about 10 minutes. Form the dough into a ball, place it in the oiled bowl, cover with a kitchen towel, and set aside for 2 hours, until doubled in size.

4. Preheat the oven to 550°F with a rack positioned in the lower third.

continues

CRUST

1½ teaspoons instant yeast

1 cup warm water (110°F to 115°F)

2¼ cups all-purpose flour, plus more for kneading

1½ teaspoons sea salt

2 tablespoons extra-virgin olive oil, plus more for greasing

SAUCE

1 (14.5-ounce) can crushed tomatoes

1 tablespoon extra-virgin olive oil

5 fresh basil leaves, roughly chopped

1 teaspoon fine sea salt

BLISTERED TOMATOES

1 cup cherry tomatoes, halved

1 tablespoon extra-virgin olive oil

½ teaspoon fine sea salt

2 garlic cloves, thinly sliced

TOPPINGS

6 ounces mozzarella cheese, cut into ½-inch cubes

2 ounces mini pepperoni slices

Freshly grated Parmesan cheese, for serving

Red pepper flakes, for serving

5. Meanwhile, make the sauce. In a medium skillet over medium heat, stir together the crushed tomatoes, olive oil, basil, and salt. Bring to a simmer, then reduce the heat to low and cook, stirring often, until the sauce thickens, about 15 minutes. Remove from the heat.

6. Brush a 12-inch cast-iron skillet with the 2 tablespoons olive oil, coating well. Turn the dough out into the skillet and use your hands to stretch the dough to the sides of the pan, being careful not to tear it. Cover the dough with a kitchen towel and set aside to rest for 20 minutes. Uncover the dough and again stretch it to the sides of the pan.

7. Meanwhile, make the blistered tomatoes. In a medium nonstick skillet, combine the cherry tomatoes, olive oil, and salt. Cook, undisturbed, until the tomatoes are blistered, about 5 minutes. Add the garlic and cook until fragrant, about 1 more minute. Transfer the tomatoes and garlic to a plate.

8. Spread about 1 cup of the pizza sauce to the edges of the pizza dough. Dot the sauce evenly with the mozzarella, all the way to the edges to ensure a lacy, crispy, cheesy crust. Top with the pepperoni, blistered tomatoes, and garlic, dispersing the toppings evenly.

9. Bake the pizza until the edges are dark brown and bubbly, about 15 minutes. Run a knife around the rim of the pizza to loosen the crust from the skillet. Carefully transfer the pizza to a cutting board. Sprinkle with Parmesan and red pepper flakes. Cut into 9 pieces and serve with any remaining sauce alongside for dipping.

CRISPY PORK LETTUCE WRAPS

Serves 4
Prep Time: 20 Minutes
Cook Time: 10 Minutes
<35 Minutes
Dairy-Free
Gluten-Free
Kid-Friendly

Just like you're not supposed to have a favorite child (and we don't), we're probably not supposed to have a favorite recipe in this book. But the truth is . . . we kind of do. Well, okay, it's not that we love it any more than the others (we're not monsters), but we are extra proud of this one. You start with pork tenderloin—and that's a good start, if ever there was one—and it just gets better from there. Slice that lean loin into thin, bite-size pieces and fry them into crispy, savory, meaty nuggets that burst with flavor and texture. Rolled up in the cooling contrast of a leaf of butter lettuce, these little wraps are our idea of complete and total bliss.

1. In a large bowl, combine the pork, cornstarch, and salt. Toss to coat well.

2. Heat the vegetable oil in a large skillet over high heat. Once the oil is glistening, working in batches as needed, add the pork and cook, undisturbed, until golden brown on the bottom, about 3 minutes. Toss and cook until crispy and golden all over, about 3 more minutes.

3. In a small bowl, stir together the soy sauce, rice vinegar, brown sugar, garlic, and ginger. Pour the sauce over the pork. Add the pineapple and white and light green onions. Cook, stirring often, until the sauce thickens and reduces slightly, about 3 minutes.

4. Spoon the pork and pineapple into the lettuce cups. Top with the cucumber and dark green onions. Sprinkle with the sesame seeds before serving.

1 pound pork tenderloin, cut into thin strips (about ½ x 3 inches)

1 tablespoon cornstarch

1 teaspoon kosher salt

1 tablespoon vegetable oil

⅓ cup low-sodium soy sauce or tamari

¼ cup rice vinegar

2 tablespoons brown sugar

3 garlic cloves, roughly chopped

2 teaspoons minced peeled fresh ginger

1 cup (½-inch cubed) fresh pineapple

3 to 4 green onions, white and light green parts thinly sliced, dark green parts reserved for garnish

1 large head butter lettuce or romaine, leaves separated

½ small English cucumber, cut into matchsticks

1 teaspoon sesame seeds

Serves 4
Prep Time: 10 Minutes
Cook Time: 15 Minutes
<35 Minutes
Dairy-Free
Gluten-Free
Sheet Pan

SUMMER VEGETABLE STEAK SALAD WITH CILANTRO LIME DRESSING

No grill, no problem. Using the broil feature on your oven (highly underrated in our opinion), you can create enough heat to give steak and veggies that char we all love so much, without checking the weather, leaving your house, or fussing around with charcoal. Start by seasoning summer veggies and steak simply with salt and pepper. Next, you'll mix up a homemade cilantro lime dressing that'll do double duty. Honey-sweetened and spiced with smoky chipotles—yet another way to bring grill vibes to this oven-cooked meal—this magical elixir swoops in and ties the entire meal together. One bite in, with raves all around, you just might find you've really outdone yourself this time.

1½ pounds skirt steak

2½ teaspoons kosher salt

1 teaspoon freshly cracked black pepper

1 medium zucchini, cut into 1-inch cubes (about 2 cups)

1 small yellow squash, cut into 1-inch cubes (about 1 cup)

½ cup plus 1 tablespoon extra-virgin olive oil

½ cup minced fresh cilantro leaves, plus more for garnish

1 to 2 chipotle peppers in adobo sauce, minced (about 2 tablespoons)

3 garlic cloves, minced

¼ cup white wine vinegar

¼ cup fresh lime juice (from 2 limes)

2 tablespoons honey

4 cups mixed greens

Note: Take the tedium out of picking herb leaves by using a fork. Rake the tines along the stem and pull the leaves through. This trick works best with leafier herbs like cilantro and parsley.

1. Turn the oven to broil with a rack positioned as close as possible to the heat source.

2. Pat the steak dry with paper towels. Season the steak all over with 1½ teaspoons of the salt and ½ teaspoon of the black pepper. Place in the center of a rimmed sheet pan.

3. In a medium bowl, toss together the zucchini, yellow squash, 1 tablespoon of the olive oil, ½ teaspoon of the salt, and the remaining ½ teaspoon black pepper.

4. In a small bowl, combine the remaining ½ cup oil, the cilantro, chipotle peppers, garlic, vinegar, lime juice, honey, and the remaining ½ teaspoon salt.

5. Brush 2 tablespoons of the cilantro lime dressing on top of the seasoned steak. Broil for 5 to 7 minutes. Remove the sheet pan from the oven. Flip the steak. Brush 2 more tablespoons of the dressing on the other side of steak. Scatter the zucchini and yellow squash all around the steak. Broil for another 5 to 7 minutes, or until the internal temperature of thickest part of the steak reaches 135°F on an instant-read thermometer for medium-rare (see Note on page 140). Remove from the oven and let rest for 5 minutes.

6. Arrange the mixed greens on a large serving platter. Add the roasted vegetables. Thinly slice the steak against the grain (see Note on page 173) and place on top. Spoon the remaining cilantro lime dressing all over and garnish with fresh cilantro. Serve family-style.

PEPPER STEAK
WITH BOK CHOY

Serves 4
Prep Time: 15 Minutes
Cook Time: 30 Minutes
Dairy-Free
Gluten-Free

Don't be intimidated by the amount of black pepper in this dish—it balances out into a slightly sweet, lightly spicy, fragrant sauce that is pure heaven when mixed with stir-fried bites of tender sirloin. It's worth mentioning, though, that in the process of stir-frying that beef, some oil may splatter a bit. If you have a splatter guard, this is your moment to use it! If you don't, and the splattering oil is getting to be too much, turn the heat down to medium as you finish frying the steak. Just remember to crank it up again to start the next batch so that the beef gets a good sear when it hits the pan.

1. Pat the steak dry with paper towels. Place the steak in a large bowl and add the salt and cornstarch. Toss to coat well.

2. Heat 1 tablespoon of the vegetable oil in a large skillet over medium-high heat. Once the oil is glistening, add the bok choy cut side down and cook undisturbed until lightly browned, about 5 minutes. Transfer to a plate.

3. Add 3 tablespoons of oil to the same skillet over medium-high heat. Once the oil is glistening, working in batches as needed, add the steak. Cook until the edges are dark brown, about 2 minutes per side, 12 to 14 minutes total. Transfer to the plate with the bok choy.

4. Add the remaining 2 tablespoons oil to the same skillet over medium-high heat. Add the shallots, garlic, and ginger and cook, stirring often, until softened, about 4 minutes. Add the soy sauce, brown sugar, and sambal oelek and cook, stirring, until the sauce thickens, about 2 minutes. Stir in the pepper and cook for another minute.

5. Return the bok choy and steak to the sauce. Stir to combine and warm through, about 2 minutes.

6. Serve the steak and bok choy over rice, if desired.

1 (1½-pound) petite sirloin, cut into 1-inch cubes

2 teaspoons kosher salt

2 tablespoons cornstarch

6 tablespoons vegetable oil

2 heads baby bok choy, quartered

3 medium shallots, halved and thinly sliced

6 garlic cloves, minced

3 tablespoons minced peeled fresh ginger (from 2 inches)

⅓ cup low-sodium soy sauce or tamari

3 tablespoons light brown sugar

1 tablespoon sambal oelek or other chili paste

2 teaspoons freshly cracked black pepper, plus more to taste

Cooked rice, for serving (optional)

Serves 4
Prep Time: 20 Minutes
Cook Time: 20 Minutes
Kid-Friendly

SKILLET-FRIED PORK CUTLETS WITH BUTTERMILK RANCH

Whoever invented Pork Milanese knew a thing or two about stress relief. Taking a mallet (or even a rolling pin) to a piece of meat and whacking it into fry-able pieces might seem like a chore at first glance, but it is, in fact, extremely satisfying. If your kids are big enough, you could outsource the work to them, but honestly, you might not want to. We don't serve our version in the traditional way—with a squeeze of lemon and a light side salad— but we did take a hint from that version in giving the pork chops a quick pan-fry and satisfying crust. But in our humble opinion, crisp meat is obviously screaming out for homemade buttermilk ranch dressing on the side. We nod in the direction of health by pairing it all with a light and crunchy apple slaw that is the perfect accompaniment.

4 (1-inch-thick) boneless pork chops (about 1½ pounds total)

1 teaspoon kosher salt

¼ teaspoon freshly cracked black pepper

2 large eggs

1½ cups panko breadcrumbs

4 tablespoons vegetable oil

2 apples, preferably Granny Smith, cut into matchsticks

2 tablespoons minced fresh chives

¾ cup Buttermilk Ranch Dressing (page 274)

Lemon wedges, for serving

1. Working with 1 pork chop at a time, place the meat between 2 sheets of parchment paper or plastic wrap. Using a meat mallet or rolling pin, pound each pork chop to ¼-inch thickness. Season the pork chops on both sides with the salt and pepper.

2. In a shallow bowl, beat the eggs. Place the panko in a separate shallow bowl. Dip each pork chop into the egg, allowing the excess to drip off. Press each pork chop into the panko to coat evenly. (See Note on dredging, page 203.)

3. Heat 2 tablespoons of the vegetable oil in a large skillet over medium heat. Once the oil is glistening, add 2 pork chops and cook, undisturbed, until golden brown on the bottom, 3 to 4 minutes. Flip the pork chops and repeat until the other side is golden brown, another 3 to 4 minutes. Add the remaining 2 tablespoons oil to the skillet and repeat with the remaining pork chops.

4. Meanwhile, combine the apples and chives in a medium bowl. Add ⅓ cup of the ranch dressing and toss to coat.

5. Add the pork and slaw to plates and squeeze fresh lemon juice over the top. Serve with the remaining ranch alongside for dipping.

CHEESY BEEF AND CARAMELIZED ONION QUESADILLA

Serves 6 to 8
Prep Time: 10 Minutes
Cook Time: 50 Minutes
Gluten-Free
Kid-Friendly

You know how people (and by "people," we mean us) are always telling you to make caramelized onions and keep them in the fridge because they're so good on everything? These beefy, cheesy quesadillas are one of those everythings! That earthy sweetness smashed on top of ground beef is a bit reminiscent of a patty melt, while a dose of BBQ spices and two kinds of cheese take this decadent dinner into a territory all its own. The finished product has a bit of a Southwestern vibe, so we like to serve them with hot sauce, avocado, jalapeños, and sour cream on the side so everyone can gussy up their own plates as they please.

1. Place the beef in a large skillet over medium-high heat. Cook, breaking it up with a wooden spoon, until browned, about 8 minutes. Transfer the beef to a colander set over a bowl to drain off the fat.

2. Return the beef to the skillet over medium heat. Add the spice rub and 2 tablespoons water and stir to combine. Cook, stirring, until the water has been absorbed, about 2 minutes. Remove the skillet from the heat.

3. Heat 1 teaspoon olive oil in a medium skillet or griddle over medium heat. Once the oil is glistening, working with one at a time, add the tortillas and sprinkle each with ¼ cup each of mozzarella, beef, caramelized onions, and cheddar, then top with another tortilla. Cook until the bottom tortilla is golden brown and the mozzarella is melted, about 3 minutes. Flip the quesadilla and cook until the other tortilla is golden brown and the cheddar is melted, about 2 more minutes. Remove from the skillet and repeat with the remaining ingredients, adding 1 teaspoon oil to the skillet for every tortilla, to make 8 quesadillas total.

4. To serve, cut each quesadilla in quarters. Serve with desired toppings.

1 pound 80/20 ground beef

¼ cup BBQ Spice Rub (page 264)

Extra-virgin olive oil

16 (10-inch) tortillas

2 cups shredded mozzarella cheese

2 cups Caramelized Onions (page 265)

2 cups shredded cheddar or colby Jack cheese

FOR SERVING

Hot sauce

Avocado

Jalapeño

Sour cream

Note: To keep these quesadillas or anything batched on the stove—like pancakes, for example—warm while you finish cooking, pop them on a sheet pan and into a 200°F oven.

Serves 2 to 4

Prep Time: 5 Minutes

Cook Time: 15 Minutes

<35 Minutes

Dairy-Free

Gluten-Free

Kid-Friendly

SWEET AND STICKY PORK AND ASPARAGUS

If you want ground pork with crispy edges—and trust us, you do—put that spatula down and don't stir your pork. Pop it in a hot pan and leave it the heck alone. Have a sip of wine or do a little dance—whatever you do, resist the temptation to mess with the meat. Let it sizzle. Let the heat and fat work their caramelization magic. In just about ten minutes, you'll be richly rewarded with a vibrant meal that's alive with texture, color, and flavor.

1 pound ground pork

½ pound asparagus, ends trimmed, cut into 2-inch pieces

¼ cup coconut aminos (see Note)

1 tablespoon sambal oelek or other chili paste

Coconut Rice (page 112) or cooked rice, for serving

Note: If you don't have coconut aminos on hand, substitute ¼ cup low-sodium soy sauce mixed with 1 tablespoon light brown sugar.

1. Heat a large nonstick skillet over medium-high heat. Add the pork and use a wooden spoon to break it up into bite-size pieces. Cook, undisturbed, until beginning to brown and crisp, about 8 minutes. Add the asparagus and cook, breaking up the meat with a wooden spoon, until the pork is cooked through and the asparagus is just tender, about 3 more minutes.

2. Stir in the coconut aminos and sambal oelek and bring to a simmer. Cook, stirring, until the pork and asparagus are coated in the sauce, 1 to 2 minutes.

3. Serve over coconut rice or plain rice.

VODKA SAUCE
BAKED GNOCCHI
WITH BABY BROCCOLI

A skillet full of pillowy potato gnocchi under a blanket of oozing mozzarella: This kind of melty, carby comfort is impossible to beat. Creamy red vodka sauce, one of our very favorites, bubbles through every crevice.

1. Preheat the oven to 400°F with a rack in the center position.

2. Bring a large pot of salted water to a boil over high heat. Add the baby broccoli and cook until bright green, about 3 minutes. Drain.

3. In the same pot, heat the olive oil over medium heat. Once the oil is glistening, add the onion and pancetta and cook, stirring occasionally, until the onion is softened and the pancetta is crispy, about 4 minutes. Add the garlic and cook until fragrant, about 1 more minute. Stir in the tomatoes and vodka. Bring the sauce to a simmer and cook until slightly reduced, 5 to 7 minutes. Stir in the Parmesan, heavy cream, and salt. Cook, stirring occasionally, until the cheese is melted and the cream is incorporated, about 5 more minutes.

4. Add the gnocchi and baby broccoli to the sauce and stir to combine. Transfer the mixture to a 12-inch ovenproof skillet or 9 x 13-inch baking dish. Scatter the mozzarella over the top.

5. Bake for about 15 minutes until the cheese is bubbly. Turn on the broiler and cook for 3 to 5 more minutes, or until the cheese is golden brown.

6. Sprinkle with the red pepper flakes, if desired, and top with more Parmesan. Serve immediately.

2 bunches baby broccoli, roughly chopped

2 tablespoons extra-virgin olive oil

1 small yellow onion, finely diced (about 1 cup)

4 ounces pancetta, diced

2 garlic cloves, minced

1 (15-ounce) can crushed tomatoes

¼ cup vodka

¾ cup freshly grated Parmesan cheese, plus more for serving

½ cup heavy cream

½ teaspoon fine sea salt

16 ounces gnocchi

1 cup shredded or torn mozzarella cheese

1 teaspoon red pepper flakes, for serving (optional)

Serves 4

Prep Time: 10 Minutes

Cook Time: 35 Minutes

Gluten-Free

Kid-Friendly

PORK CHOPS WITH CHARRED PEPPERS

Never made roasted peppers before? Now is your chance! Roasted peppers taste good on virtually everything, and they're incredibly easy to make. You don't need any special tools or skills—just your broiler and a little patience. We say patience because totally blackened skin is a must on these peppers, and that takes a bit of time. You want to let the peppers char deeply so that even when you slip off the skins, you can see some char on the flesh. It imparts the smoky flavor we're after and is the element that makes this otherwise pretty basic pork chop dinner totally memorable.

2 medium red bell peppers, halved and seeded

1 medium yellow bell pepper, halved and seeded

1 medium orange bell pepper, halved and seeded

4 (1- to 1½-inch-thick) bone-in pork chops (2 to 2½ pounds total)

3 teaspoons kosher salt

1½ teaspoons freshly cracked black pepper

2 tablespoons vegetable oil

¼ cup packed chopped fresh basil leaves

2 tablespoons toasted pine nuts

2 tablespoons white wine vinegar

½ cup Basil Pesto (page 267), at room temperature

1. Turn on the broiler with a rack in the center position. Line a rimmed sheet pan with foil.

2. Arrange the peppers, cut sides down, on the prepared sheet pan. Broil, rotating the pan at least once, until the tops of the peppers are completely charred, 8 to 10 minutes. Remove from the oven and let cool.

3. Meanwhile, pat the pork chops dry with paper towels. Season all over with 2½ teaspoons of the salt and 1 teaspoon of the pepper.

4. Heat the vegetable oil in a large skillet over high heat. Once the oil just begins smoking, reduce the heat to medium. Working in two batches, add the pork chops. Cook, undisturbed, for 3 minutes, then flip and continue cooking for another 3 minutes. Continue cooking this way, flipping the pork, until the internal temperature of the pork reads 140°F to 150°F on an instant-read thermometer (see page 29), 12 to 16 minutes total (depending on the thickness of the pork chops). Transfer the pork chops to a serving platter and cover with foil to keep warm. Repeat with remaining pork chops.

5. Peel away the skins from the bell peppers and discard. Slice the peppers into thin strips and place them in a medium bowl. Add the basil, pine nuts, vinegar, the remaining ½ teaspoon salt, and the remaining ½ teaspoon black pepper. Toss to combine.

6. Spoon the charred pepper salad over the pork chops. Drizzle the pesto over the top and serve family-style.

CRISPY CARNITAS

Serves 6 to 8
Prep Time: 15 Minutes
Cook Time: 3 Hours 20 Minutes
Dairy-Free
Gluten-Free
Kid-Friendly

Economical and versatile, pork shoulder is a workhorse and carnitas is our absolute favorite way to cook it. We season this tough, fatty cut with a few warm spices and some citrus and let low, slow heat work its tenderizing magic. When the carnitas are done, the sky's the limit as to what you can make with it. Start with tacos the first night, and use the leftovers—and you *will* have leftovers—in a breakfast hash the next morning, or in a lunchtime quesadilla. We also think a batch of hearty, aromatic, juicy carnitas acts as the ultimate camping or cabin trip make-ahead. Whip up a batch before you go, and you have the base for at least a few days' worth of super-easy, please-everyone meals.

1 cup chicken stock

1 medium yellow onion, quartered

1 large orange, juiced, rind reserved

Juice of 1 lime

2 teaspoons dried oregano

2 teaspoons chili powder

2 teaspoons kosher salt

2 teaspoons ground cumin

1 teaspoon freshly cracked black pepper

¼ teaspoon cayenne pepper

2 bay leaves

3 pounds boneless pork shoulder, cut into 4 pieces

1. Preheat the oven to 375°F with a rack in the center position.

2. In a large Dutch oven, combine the chicken stock, onion, orange juice and rind, lime juice, oregano, chili powder, salt, cumin, black pepper, cayenne, and bay leaves. Place the pot over high heat and bring to a boil.

3. Nestle in the meat, cover, and roast for 2½ to 3 hours, until the pork is very tender and can be pulled apart easily with a fork. Using a slotted spoon, transfer the pork to a large baking dish or rimmed sheet pan, discarding any large pieces of fat. Return the Dutch oven to high heat. Bring the liquid to a boil and cook until reduced by two thirds, about 20 minutes.

4. Meanwhile, use two forks to shred the pork into 1-inch pieces. Once the liquid has reduced, generously brush the meat with it.

5. Turn on the broiler. Broil the shredded meat until the edges are crispy and caramelized, about 5 minutes. Remove the baking dish from the oven and using a spatula, flip the meat over. Broil for 5 more minutes, or until crispy on top.

6. Use the carnitas as desired. Store in an airtight container in the refrigerator for up to 1 week or in the freezer for up to 1 month.

Serves 6

Prep Time: 15 Minutes

Cook Time: 25 Minutes

Dairy-Free

Gluten-Free

Kid-Friendly

CARNITAS BURRITO BOWL WITH CORN SALSA

Carnitas are not just for stuffing tacos or eating straight out of the pan! If you have some left over, this bowl is ideal for using them up. It's also tasty enough that you might want to make a batch of that succulent Mexican-style pulled pork solely so that you can eat this dish for dinner. The spicy corn salsa slices right through the richness of the tender meat, and its juices seep into the lime-cilantro rice for a meal that'll really knock your socks off. We love to finish this bowl with avocado, but make it your own with hot sauce or whatever other toppings sound most delicious—there's no wrong way to carnitas.

RICE

2 cups long-grain white rice, rinsed (see Note on page 112)

2 tablespoons vegetable oil

1 teaspoon kosher salt, plus more to taste

⅓ cup finely chopped fresh cilantro

1 teaspoon grated lime zest

1 tablespoon fresh lime juice (from 1 lime)

SALSA

3 ears corn (or 2 cups frozen corn, thawed; see Note on page 116)

¼ cup finely chopped red onion (from 1 small red onion)

1 medium jalapeño, seeded and finely chopped

¼ cup finely chopped fresh cilantro

1 tablespoon fresh lime juice (from 1 lime)

½ teaspoon kosher salt

2 cups Carnitas (page 161), warmed

Sliced avocado, for serving

1. **Make the rice.** In a medium saucepan, combine the rice, 2½ cups water, the vegetable oil, and the salt. Bring to a boil over high heat. Reduce the heat to low, cover, and cook until the rice is cooked through and the water has been absorbed, about 20 minutes. Uncover and fluff with a fork. Stir in the cilantro and lime zest and juice. Season with salt to taste.

2. **Meanwhile, make the salsa.** Bring a large pot of water to a boil over high heat. Add the corn and cook until just tender, about 3 minutes. Drain and rinse until the ears are just cool enough to handle. Slice the kernels off the cob and place in a large bowl. Add the onion, jalapeño, cilantro, lime juice, and salt and combine well.

3. To serve, divide the rice among 6 bowls. Top with the carnitas, corn salsa, and avocado.

STEAK SANDWICH WITH HORSERADISH MAYO

Serves 4
Prep Time: 10 Minutes
Cook Time: 20 Minutes
<35 Minutes

There are sandwiches you scarf down between meetings, and then there are sandwiches so good you plan your whole day around them. These over-the-top baguette masterpieces are the latter. Make a mess of them—they're ideal for serving a small crowd—and take them to the park for a truly decadent picnic. You can even make them a day ahead of time, if need be—just leave the arugula off until the very last minute.

1. Pat the steak dry. Season both sides with the kosher salt. Heat the olive oil in a large cast-iron skillet over high heat. Once the oil is glistening, add the steak and cook, undisturbed, for 2 minutes. Flip the steak and cook for 2 more minutes. Continue cooking this way until the internal temperature of the steak reaches 135°F on an instant-read thermometer for medium-rare, 10 to 12 minutes total (see Note on page 140). Transfer the steak to a plate and let rest for 10 minutes. Slice the steak as thin as possible against the grain (see Note on page 173).

2. Turn on the broiler. Cut the baguette into 4 equal pieces, then halve each piece crosswise. Arrange the bread, cut side up, on a rimmed sheet pan and broil until just toasted, 2 to 3 minutes.

3. In a small bowl, stir together the mayonnaise and horseradish.

4. Spread the horseradish mayonnaise on the inside of each piece of bread. On half of the pieces, layer the arugula, Brie, sliced steak, and red onion, dividing evenly. Season to taste with flaky salt and pepper. Top with the remaining slices of bread and serve.

1 pound flank steak

1 tablespoon kosher salt

1 tablespoon extra-virgin olive oil

1 (12-inch) baguette

¼ cup mayonnaise

3 tablespoons prepared horseradish

1 cup loosely packed arugula

4 ounces Brie cheese, sliced

¼ small red onion, thinly sliced

Flaky salt

Freshly cracked black pepper

Serves 6

Prep Time: 15 Minutes

Cook Time: 25 Minutes

Dairy-Free

Gluten-Free

Kid-Friendly

BEEF SKEWERS

½ cup full-fat coconut milk, shaken before measuring

4 garlic cloves, minced

2 tablespoons chopped fresh cilantro, plus more for garnish

2 tablespoons light brown sugar

2 tablespoons fish sauce

1 tablespoon ground turmeric

½ teaspoon kosher salt

2 pounds skirt steak, thinly sliced against the grain (see Note on page 173)

CUCUMBER SALAD

6 small Persian cucumbers, cut into 2-inch pieces

4 green onions, white and green parts, thinly sliced

½ cup rice vinegar

⅓ cup granulated sugar

2 tablespoons toasted sesame oil

1 teaspoon red pepper flakes

½ teaspoon kosher salt

¼ cup crushed peanuts, for serving

Peanut Sauce (page 275), for serving

Notes: If you freeze your beef for an hour or two before slicing it, you'll get much better results. This trick works great for chicken too!

A grill pan is a great indoor alternative to a grill. Use it over high heat on your stovetop—just note that it won't take quite as long to heat up as the grill, so no need to worry about it until after your skewers are threaded and ready. Brush it with some olive oil to avoid sticking.

BEEF SATAY WITH SMASHED CUCUMBER SALAD

In Southeast Asian cuisine, "satay" refers to the style in which meat is cooked: marinated, skewered, then grilled and served with some kind of dipping sauce that's often, but not always, peanut-based. We love a great peanut sauce, and, to be honest, we think our version is pretty great—it may or may not be what pulls this dish together. It makes for a terrific family-style appetizer, or you can turn it into a hearty bowl by serving it over, you guessed it, steamed white rice. Sometimes we don't so much "serve" these as just eat the skewers straight off the grill!

1. **Make the beef.** In a large bowl, stir together the coconut milk, garlic, cilantro, brown sugar, fish sauce, turmeric, and salt. Add the beef and turn to coat. Cover and let marinate in the refrigerator for at least 2 hours or up to overnight.

2. Preheat the grill on high (see Notes). Remove the steak from the marinade, allowing any excess to drip off. Weave the steak lengthwise through metal or soaked bamboo skewers, dividing evenly. Place the skewers on the grill or grill pan (see Notes) and cook without moving them for 2 minutes. Flip and continue cooking just until the beef is crispy on the edges, about 2 more minutes.

3. **Meanwhile, make the salad.** Using the side of a knife, smash the cucumber pieces. Place the cucumber in a medium bowl. Add the green onions, rice vinegar, sugar, sesame oil, red pepper flakes, and salt. Toss to combine, then set aside for about 10 minutes to allow the flavors to meld.

4. Arrange the skewers on a large platter. Garnish with cilantro and the crushed peanuts. Serve the beef satay with the cucumber salad and peanut sauce alongside.

EVERYTHING BAGEL SAUSAGE FRIED RICE

Serves 4
Prep Time: 5 Minutes
Cook Time: 15 Minutes
<35 Minutes
Dairy-Free
Gluten-Free
Kid-Friendly

Everything bagel seasoning, rice, eggs, sausage. On paper, none of it seems to go together, but trust us when we say it just works. The smokiness of the sausage gets along well with the oniony bits in the bagel seasoning. Add some eggs and some rice and it all comes together. If you've never gotten the hang of making fried rice, here's the big secret: You want to use day-old rice—two or three days old is even better. It's the key to getting those perfectly crispy bits. If you don't have day-old rice, no problem. Spread out some freshly cooked rice on a rimmed sheet pan and let it dry for an hour or two.

1. In a large skillet over medium-high heat, cook the sliced sausage until crispy on both sides, about 4 minutes total. Transfer the sausage to a plate.

2. In the same skillet, heat 3 tablespoons of the vegetable oil over medium-high heat. Once the oil is glistening, add the rice and toss to coat. Spread the rice evenly on the bottom of the pan. Cook, undisturbed, until the rice begins to crisp on the bottom, 2 to 3 minutes. Stir the rice once, then continue to cook, undisturbed, until slightly crispy, another 2 to 3 minutes. Transfer the rice to the plate with the sausage.

3. Add the remaining 1 tablespoon oil to the skillet and reduce the heat to medium. Add the eggs and cook, scrambling, until set, about 1 minute.

4. Return the sausage and rice to the skillet. Add the green onions and seasoning. Cook, stirring, to combine and warm through, 1 to 2 minutes.

5. Serve the fried rice topped with more seasoning.

1 pound cooked smoked sausage links, cut into ¼-inch-thick slices

4 tablespoons vegetable oil

4 cups cooked white rice, preferably day-old

2 large eggs, beaten

4 green onions, white and green parts, thinly sliced

2 tablespoons Everything Bagel Seasoning (page 264), plus more for garnish

Serves 6
Prep Time: 15 Minutes
Cook Time: 30 Minutes
Gluten-Free
Kid-Friendly

GARLIC BUTTER STEAK STIR-FRY WITH SNAP PEAS

Easy. Steak. Butter. Garlic. We have your attention now, right? Crispy, sweet snow peas and a fragrant sauce are the perfect match for this beefy stir-fry. While you can use flat iron or skirt steak, lean, meaty flank steak is our very favorite for this speedy dinner. If you're avoiding grains, it can stand alone as dinner. If you're not, we highly recommend serving this over steamed rice or, perhaps even better, with udon or soba noodles.

2 pounds flank, skirt, or flat iron steak, cut against the grain into ¼-inch-thick strips (see Note on page 173)

1 teaspoon kosher salt

½ teaspoon freshly cracked black pepper

¼ cup low-sodium soy sauce or tamari

2 tablespoons cornstarch

1 tablespoon vegetable oil

¼ cup beef or chicken stock

4 tablespoons (½ stick) salted butter

4 garlic cloves, minced

3 cups snap peas, trimmed (8 ounces)

3 green onions, white and green parts, thinly sliced (optional)

Finely chopped fresh flat-leaf parsley leaves (optional)

Cooked rice, for serving (optional)

1. Season the steak all over with the salt and pepper.

2. In a medium bowl, stir together the soy sauce and cornstarch. Add the steak and toss to coat evenly with the marinade.

3. Heat the vegetable oil in a large cast-iron skillet or wok over high heat. Once the oil is just smoking, working in batches, add the steak in a single layer and cook, undisturbed, until slightly crispy, 1 to 2 minutes per side. Transfer to a plate and continue with the remaining steak.

4. Reduce the heat to medium. Add the stock, butter, and garlic and bring to a simmer. Cook, scraping up any browned bits from the bottom, until the garlic is fragrant, 2 to 3 minutes. Add the snap peas and cook, stirring occasionally, until beginning to soften, about 2 more minutes.

5. Return the steak and any collected juices to the pan. Add the green onions and parsley, if desired. Toss to combine. Serve warm over rice, if desired.

Note: Overcrowding a pan—on top of the stove or in the oven—can mean steaming instead of searing or crisping. That's why spacing things out and working in small batches can be key.

CREAMY MUSTARD SAUCE BUCATINI WITH STEAK AND ASPARAGUS

Serves 4 to 6
Prep Time: 10 Minutes
Cook Time: 25 Minutes
<35 Minutes
Kid-Friendly

White wine, garlic, and mustard lend plenty of warmth and zip to a superbly basic cream sauce that partners best with thick, hollow twirls of bucatini. If you can't find bucatini, though, any long pasta will work. Crown those irresistible noodles with seared skirt steak—we like ours nice and tender—and springy asparagus, and you have a dinner that's just begging to be enjoyed outside on one of those first glorious warm, balmy nights of the year.

1. Fill a large pot with 4 quarts water and add 2 teaspoons of the salt. Bring to a boil over high heat. Add the asparagus and cook until bright green, about 3 minutes. Using tongs or a slotted spoon, transfer the asparagus to a paper towel–lined plate, reserving the boiling water on the stove.

2. To the boiling water, add the pasta and cook, according to the package directions, to al dente. Drain.

3. Meanwhile, heat the olive oil in a large cast-iron skillet over medium-high heat. Season the steak with ½ teaspoon of the salt and ¼ teaspoon of the pepper. Once the oil is glistening, add the steak and cook until the internal temperature reads 135°F on an instant-read thermometer for medium-rare, about 5 minutes per side, depending on the thickness (see Note on page 140). Transfer the steak to a cutting board. Let rest for 5 minutes, then thinly slice against the grain (see Note).

4. In the same skillet, melt the butter over medium heat. Add the garlic and cook, scraping up any browned bits from the bottom, until fragrant, about 1 minute. Add the wine and cook until reduced by half, about 2 minutes. Add the mustard, cream, remaining ½ teaspoon salt, and remaining ¼ teaspoon pepper. Cook, whisking, until the sauce is thickened, about 5 minutes. Taste and adjust the salt as needed.

5. Add the pasta to the sauce in the skillet and toss to coat. Serve the pasta with the steak and asparagus over the top.

3 teaspoons kosher salt

½ pound asparagus, ends trimmed, cut into 3-inch pieces

¾ pound bucatini pasta

1 tablespoon extra-virgin olive oil

1 pound skirt steak

½ teaspoon freshly cracked black pepper

2 tablespoons unsalted butter

4 garlic cloves, thinly sliced

¾ cup dry white wine, such as sauvignon blanc

2 tablespoons whole-grain mustard

1 cup heavy cream

Note: You always want to slice steak against the grain to ensure every bite is as tender as can be. Look closely for the parallel lines running down the meat—these are the muscle fibers—and slice perpendicular to them, rather than along them.

Serves 6
Prep Time: 15 Minutes
Cook Time: 2 Hours 30 Minutes
Dairy-Free
Gluten-Free
Kid-Friendly

POT ROAST

Tomatoes, lots of garlic, wine, and pancetta give this otherwise classic pot roast its Italian accent. We like to sear our meat before cooking it low and slow—and unlike in a traditional roast, we cut it into perfect portions so that everyone gets to enjoy those crispy edges. Maybe the weather's a bit dreary. Maybe you'd like your house to smell really, really good. Maybe you're craving an old-fashioned Sunday family dinner. Whatever the reason—or maybe it's all of the above—this big pot of rich comfort will deliver, every time.

1 (3-pound) chuck roast, fat trimmed, cut into approximately 3-inch pieces

1 tablespoon kosher salt

2 teaspoons freshly cracked black pepper

2 tablespoons extra-virgin olive oil

4 ounces pancetta or good-quality bacon, diced

1 small yellow onion, finely chopped

2 large carrots, peeled and diced

2 to 3 celery ribs, finely chopped

6 garlic cloves, minced

2 tablespoons tomato paste

2 cups light red wine, such as pinot noir

2 bay leaves

2 sprigs fresh thyme

Finely chopped fresh flat-leaf parsley leaves, for serving

Mashed potatoes or cooked egg noodles, for serving

1. Preheat the oven to 350°F with a rack in the center position.

2. Generously season the beef all over with the salt and pepper. Heat the olive oil in a Dutch oven over medium-high heat. Once the oil just begins to smoke, working in batches, add the meat and cook until browned, 2 to 3 minutes per side. Transfer the meat to a plate.

3. Reduce the heat to medium. Add the pancetta and cook, stirring occasionally, until it crisps and the fat has rendered, 3 to 4 minutes. Add the onion, carrots, and celery, and cook, stirring constantly, until softened, about 5 minutes. If the vegetables are sticking to the bottom of the pot, add a bit of water and scrape up the browned bits. Add the garlic and cook, stirring, until fragrant, about 1 more minute. Stir in the tomato paste to combine. Pour in the wine and stir to incorporate.

4. Return the meat to the pan along with any collected juices, nestling it in but not submerging it. Add the bay leaves and thyme. Increase the heat to high and bring to a boil, then cover the pot and transfer it to the oven. Cook for about 2 hours, or until the meat is tender and shreds easily with a fork. Discard the bay leaves and thyme stems. Using tongs, transfer the meat to a serving platter and tent with foil to keep warm.

5. Return the pan to medium-high heat and bring the liquid to a boil. Cook until reduced by about a third, 8 to 10 minutes. Pour the sauce over the meat on the platter. Garnish with parsley.

6. Serve the pot roast family-style with mashed potatoes or egg noodles alongside.

WEEKNIGHT SORT-OF-CASSOULET

Serves 4 to 6
Prep Time: 5 Minutes
Cook Time: 45 Minutes
Dairy-Free
Gluten-Free
Kid-Friendly

Julia Child described cassoulet as "French baked beans," and it's as much a perfect description as it is a vast oversimplification. At its most basic, cassoulet is simply white beans baked super slowly with meat and herbs. As with many old, iconic dishes, there's a fair amount of argument about what ingredients must be included in a "true" cassoulet, but we favor a version that can be made quickly enough to enjoy on a busy weeknight. Now, that might sound like sacrilege to cassoulet purists. But sometimes we just want to feel transported to the French countryside with a hearty bowl of beans and sausage on a Tuesday night. Pro tip: Pair it with a glass of Côtes du Rhône to seal the deal.

1. Preheat the oven to 400°F with a rack in the center position.

2. Heat the olive oil in a 12-inch ovenproof skillet over medium heat. Once the oil is glistening, add the sausages and cook, turning, until browned, about 5 minutes per side. Transfer the sausages to a plate.

3. Add the onion to the same skillet over medium heat and cook, stirring, until beginning to soften, about 4 minutes. Add the garlic and cook, stirring, until fragrant, about 1 more minute.

4. Add the wine and simmer, scraping up any brown bits as you stir, until the liquid is almost all evaporated, about 3 minutes. Add the tomatoes, chicken stock, basil, thyme, salt, and pepper and simmer until the sauce has reduced by half, about 10 minutes. Stir in the beans and nestle in the sausages.

5. Transfer the skillet to the oven and bake for 15 minutes, or until the internal temperature of the sausage reaches 165°F on an instant-read thermometer.

6. Garnish with more fresh basil and serve family-style with crusty bread alongside.

1 tablespoon extra-virgin olive oil

1 pound mild Italian sausage (4 links)

1 medium yellow onion, diced

3 garlic cloves, minced

½ cup dry white wine, such as sauvignon blanc

1 (15-ounce) can crushed tomatoes

1 cup chicken stock

¼ cup fresh basil leaves, thinly sliced, plus more for garnish

4 sprigs fresh thyme

1 teaspoon kosher salt

½ teaspoon freshly cracked black pepper

2 (15-ounce) cans Great Northern beans, drained and rinsed

Crusty bread, for serving (optional)

Serves 6
Prep Time: 10 Minutes
Cook Time: 20 Minutes
<35 Minutes
Gluten-Free
Kid-Friendly
Sheet Pan

1 pound 80/20 ground beef

½ medium red onion, finely chopped

1 jalapeño, seeded and minced

¼ cup Taco Seasoning (page 267)

1 (16-ounce) can refried beans

1 (15-ounce) bag tortilla chips

3 cups shredded cheddar cheese

OPTIONAL TOPPINGS
Finely chopped fresh cilantro
Pickled jalapeños, drained
Guacamole or sliced avocado
Sour cream
Finely chopped red onion
Pico de gallo
Salsa

MOM'S NACHOS

Quite possibly the ultimate snacky meal, this version of nachos doesn't differ much from the one Holly's mom served when she was a kid. All we've done is swap in our homemade taco seasoning for store-bought—the rest is all Mom's. Stirring the seasoned beef and beans together is kind of a game changer, and layering it with the chips and cheese multiple times ensures every bite is loaded with melty, meaty goodness. Whether it's game night or family movie night, this decidedly unfancy tray-o-nachos hits the spot like none other.

1. Preheat the oven to 400°F with a rack in the center position.

2. In a large skillet over medium-high heat, combine the beef, red onion, and minced jalapeño. Cook, breaking up the meat with a spoon, until the meat is browned, about 8 minutes. Sprinkle in the taco seasoning and stir to combine. Stir in the beans and cook until combined and heated through, 2 to 3 minutes.

3. Spread out half of the tortilla chips on a rimmed sheet pan. Dollop evenly with one third of the meat and bean mixture and sprinkle one third of the cheese over the top. Layer on the remaining chips, the remaining beef and bean mixture, and the remaining shredded cheese.

4. Bake for 5 to 7 minutes, or until the top layer of cheese is fully melted. Add toppings as desired and serve.

SEAFOOD

Serves 4

Prep Time: 15 Minutes

Cook Time: 15 Minutes

<35 Minutes

Dairy-Free

Gluten-Free

PAN-SEARED SHRIMP WITH BURST CURRY TOMATOES

We don't need to sell you on shrimp—with their ability to go from frozen to finished quickly, it's no wonder we love the crustaceans. Seafood always demands a lighter sauce, but that doesn't mean you can't use a few carefully chosen big flavors. Here, we've taken the ever-lovable cherry tomato, whose ability to collapse into a silky sauce is one of its very best qualities. Garlic, and lots of it, is a classic partner for both shrimp and tomatoes, so we've thrown that into the mix, too (we're pretty sure you can never have enough of it). With a dash of curry powder and a fistful of cilantro, you have a vibrant dish that's as delicious as it is show-stoppingly beautiful.

4 tablespoons extra-virgin olive oil

1 pound large, tail-on raw shrimp, peeled and deveined

2 pints cherry tomatoes

6 garlic cloves, thinly sliced

1 tablespoon yellow curry powder

¾ teaspoon kosher salt

¼ teaspoon ground allspice

¼ teaspoon freshly cracked black pepper

¼ cup minced fresh cilantro leaves

Flatbread or naan, for serving

Cooked rice, for serving

1. Heat 2 tablespoons of the olive oil in a medium skillet over medium-high heat. Once the oil is glistening, add the shrimp and cook, undisturbed, until just pink on the bottom, about 1½ minutes. Flip and cook on the other side until pink, opaque, and cooked through, about 1 more minute. Using a slotted spoon, transfer the shrimp to a plate.

2. Add the remaining 2 tablespoons oil to the same skillet over high heat. Add the cherry tomatoes and cook, undisturbed, until beginning to blister, about 5 minutes. Add the garlic and continue cooking, stirring occasionally, until the garlic is golden brown and the tomatoes begin to burst, about 5 more minutes. Add the curry, salt, allspice, and pepper and cook, stirring, until fragrant, about 2 minutes.

3. Return the shrimp to the skillet. Stir in the cilantro. Transfer the mixture to a serving platter and serve with flatbread and rice alongside.

ANY KIND OF
FISH CAKES WITH
RED PEPPER AIOLI

Serves 4
Prep Time: 15 Minutes
Cook Time: 20 Minutes
<35 Minutes
Dairy-Free

When Natalie was growing up, her mom would often make a simple roast fish (usually salmon) for dinner, and if there were leftovers, everyone knew fish cakes would be on the menu the next night. That's why we call this recipe "any kind of fish" cakes—it is simple enough that it works with any fish from tinned tuna to wild crab to last night's leftover salmon and everything in between. We've swapped out Mom's preferred Ritz crackers for panko because we love the lightness and crunch. Serve these cakes with this super easy dump-and-blend red pepper aioli, or they're delicious with Tartar Sauce (page 207), too. Add a side salad and dinner is done.

1. **Make the aioli.** In the base of a food processor, combine the mayonnaise, red peppers, garlic, paprika, and salt. Blend until smooth, about 2 minutes. Cover and refrigerate.

2. **Make the fish cakes.** Place the fish in a large bowl. Use a fork to flake the fish into small bite-size pieces. Fold in the eggs until just combined. Add 1 cup of the panko, the celery, green onions, Dijon, Old Bay, salt, and pepper. Gently fold until just combined.

3. Using your hands, carefully form the fish mixture into patties about 3 inches wide and 1 inch thick. You should have 6 to 8 patties. Place the remaining ½ cup panko on a plate. Gently press the patties into the panko to create a crust all over.

4. Pour ¼ inch vegetable oil into a large skillet. Heat over medium-high heat. Once the oil is glistening, working in batches, add the fish cakes in a single layer, being careful not to overcrowd, and cook until just golden brown on the bottom, about 3 minutes. Flip and cook until the other side is golden brown, about 3 more minutes. Remove from the skillet and keep warm in the oven (see Note on page 155). Repeat with the remaining fish cakes, adding more oil to the skillet as needed to maintain ¼ inch.

5. Arrange the fish cakes on a serving platter. Add lemon wedges for squeezing. Serve with the red pepper aioli alongside.

AIOLI
½ cup mayonnaise
¼ cup jarred roasted red peppers, drained
1 garlic clove, smashed
1 teaspoon smoked paprika
½ teaspoon fine sea salt

FISH CAKES
1 pound cooked fish, such as salmon, tuna, cod, or crab
2 large eggs, beaten
1½ cups panko breadcrumbs
1 celery rib, minced (about ¼ cup)
3 green onions, white and green parts, minced (about ¼ cup)
2 teaspoons Dijon mustard
2 teaspoons Old Bay seasoning
½ teaspoon fine sea salt
¼ teaspoon freshly cracked black pepper
Vegetable oil, for frying
Lemon wedges, for serving

Serves 2 to 4
Prep Time: 15 Minutes
Cook Time: 15 Minutes
<35 Minutes
Gluten-Free

WHITE FISH IN ORANGE BUTTER SAUCE

We truly believe there's a white fish for every taste. If you like mild and meaty, halibut is probably your jam. A little more oceanic assertiveness? You might be more of a snapper person. Firm, flaky, and affordable? Try cod! Whatever your preference, this elegant, classic, quick way of cooking will let the fillet shine. If you don't have herb butter at the ready, you can make do with salted butter, but we urge you to take the extra few minutes to mix up that herby goodness. It really does take this recipe from good to stupendous, and with very little extra effort. Rinsing the olives before adding them to the pan might seem a bit odd, but because olives are quite salty on their own, you don't want to risk any of their briny oil creating an oversalted situation.

½ cup Herb Butter (page 276) or ½ cup (1 stick) salted butter

1 small shallot, finely diced

2 tablespoons grated orange zest

2 tablespoons fresh orange juice

1 teaspoon white wine vinegar

1 pound white fish, such as cod, halibut, or sea bass, skin removed, cut into 4 pieces

1 cup pitted Castelvetrano olives, rinsed and smashed

Freshly cracked black pepper

Notes: Spooning butter over the fish—called basting—is best achieved by carefully tipping the pan so the butter pools a bit and is easier to get to.

If your pieces of fish are thicker than 1 inch, flip them halfway through cooking and test for flakiness beginning at 8 minutes.

1. Heat half of the butter in a medium skillet over medium heat. Once the butter is melted and beginning to bubble, add the shallot and cook, stirring occasionally, until translucent, about 3 minutes.

2. Add the orange zest and juice, vinegar, and the remaining butter. Once the butter has melted, add the fish. Cook, occasionally spooning the butter over the fish, until the fish is opaque and flaky, 8 to 10 minutes (see Notes). Add the olives and cook until just warmed through, about 1 minute. Season with pepper to taste.

ROASTED HONEY MUSTARD SALMON WITH CITRUS SALAD

Serves 4 to 6
Prep Time: 20 Minutes
Cook Time: 15 Minutes
<35 Minutes
Dairy-Free
Gluten-Free

One of our favorite "secrets" is that most salad dressings happily do double duty as seasonings for meat—fish and chicken, especially. Honey mustard vinaigrette is one such dressing and we particularly love its sweet-tartness not only as the marinade, as in this dish, but also drizzled over simply baked salmon. It cuts through the fattiness of this beloved fish, and a hint of sweetness means even non–fish lovers are more likely to give it a go. As for this citrus salad, a sharp knife makes quick work of removing the peel. Then it's up to you whether you'd like to supreme the citrus into wedges or slice it into rounds. Either way, it'll be a festival of sunset hues that will play perfectly off the pink of the salmon, making for a dinner that's almost too pretty to eat—almost.

1. **Make the salmon.** Preheat the oven to 375°F. Line a rimmed sheet pan with parchment paper.

2. Place the salmon on the prepared sheet pan. Season with the salt and with pepper to taste. Brush the vinaigrette all over the salmon, then sprinkle it with the pistachios.

3. Bake for 12 to 15 minutes (depending on thickness), or until the fish flakes easily with a fork.

4. **Meanwhile, make the salad.** Using a small paring knife, trim the tops and bottoms off the citrus so that they sit flat. Carefully trim the peel off just enough to expose the fruit while removing as much of the white pith as possible. From here, either supreme the fruit by cutting out each wedge from the membranes, or slice into rounds.

5. Assemble the salad on each plate by layering the grapefruit, oranges, and avocado. Dress lightly with the vinaigrette. Sprinkle the pistachios and shallot over the top. Place the salmon on top of the salad and serve.

SALMON
1 (1½-pound) salmon fillet
1 teaspoon fine sea salt
Freshly cracked black pepper
2 tablespoons Honey Mustard Vinaigrette (page 272)
¼ cup finely chopped unsalted pistachios

SALAD
1 large grapefruit
2 medium oranges
1 avocado, sliced
½ cup Honey Mustard Vinaigrette (page 272)
1 tablespoon finely chopped unsalted pistachios
1 small shallot, minced

Serves 4
Prep Time: 15 Minutes
Cook Time: 15 Minutes
<35 Minutes
Gluten-Free

FISH TACOS

Light and bursting with freshness, fish tacos are a taste of summer that's welcome any time of year in our homes. Simple white fish—use whatever's easily available—is a mild base for a slew of zesty, herbal toppings that add up to a dish full of Southwestern flair. A squeeze of lime and a good dose of BBQ seasoning liven up a sour cream–based sauce that plays well with the crunchy onion-and-cabbage slaw it gets tossed with. (Trust us: Whatever you do, do not skip that slaw.) A little avocado, some cilantro . . . pile it all into a warm tortilla and dig in.

1 tablespoon extra-virgin olive oil

1 pound white fish, such as cod or tilapia, skin removed

5 tablespoons BBQ Spice Rub (page 264)

¼ cup sour cream

¼ cup mayonnaise

2 tablespoons fresh lime juice (from 1 to 2 limes)

3 cups shredded green cabbage (about 9 ounces)

⅓ cup thinly sliced white onion (½ medium onion)

⅓ cup chopped fresh cilantro leaves

6 to 8 (6-inch) corn tortillas, warmed

Sliced avocado, for serving (optional)

Mexican hot sauce, for serving (optional)

Lime wedges, for serving

1. Preheat the oven to 375°F. Line a rimmed sheet pan with parchment paper.

2. Drizzle the olive oil over the prepared sheet pan. Add the fish and sprinkle on both sides with 3 tablespoons of the spice rub. Bake for 5 minutes. Turn on the broiler and continue baking for 5 to 7 more minutes, until the fish is opaque and slightly browned on the edges.

3. Meanwhile, in a small bowl, combine the sour cream, mayonnaise, lime juice, and the remaining 2 tablespoons spice rub. Stir to mix well. Transfer half of the mixture to a large bowl. Add the cabbage, onion, and cilantro. Toss to coat.

4. Flake the fish into bite-size pieces and divide it evenly among the tortillas. Add the cabbage slaw and then avocado, hot sauce, and the remaining sour cream mixture, if desired. Serve the tacos with lime wedges for squeezing.

SWEET CIDER SCALLOPS WITH WILTED SPINACH

Serves 4
Prep Time: 5 Minutes
Cook Time: 25 minutes
<35 Minutes
Gluten-Free

Raisins and a kiss of maple syrup give this dish a gentle sweetness, but that is balanced by a hit of acid from cider vinegar and plenty of spicy, fresh garlic and smoky paprika. If all of that sounds like it might overwhelm the buttery delicate flavor of sea scallops, fear not. Your investment—and we know, good scallops are just that—is safe with us. Inspired by a dish Natalie first had at a Spanish restaurant, and re-created from memory on an idyllic rare day alone in the kitchen—minus the kids, plus the rosé—this medley of ingredients is neither too much nor too little, and it's not too complicated either. In fact, it's just right.

1. Pat the scallops dry and season them with 1 teaspoon of the salt, the paprika, and the pepper.

2. Heat 1 tablespoon of the butter and 1 tablespoon of the olive oil together in a large skillet over medium-high heat. Once the butter is melted and the oil is glistening, working in batches as needed, add the scallops in a single layer. Cook, undisturbed, until golden brown on the bottom, 4 to 5 minutes. Flip and continue cooking until opaque and cooked through, another 3 to 4 minutes. Transfer the scallops to a plate.

3. Wipe out the skillet and return it to medium-low heat. Add the vinegar and 2 tablespoons water and bring to a simmer. Add the raisins and cook, undisturbed, until the raisins are plump and the liquid has evaporated, about 3 minutes. Transfer the raisins to a separate plate.

4. Add the remaining 2 tablespoons butter and 2 tablespoons oil to the skillet over medium heat. Once the butter is melted and the oil is glistening, add the garlic and cook, stirring occasionally, until golden brown, about 2 minutes. Add the spinach and maple syrup. Cook, stirring occasionally, until the spinach is just wilted, about 2 minutes. Return the plumped raisins to the pan and add the remaining ½ teaspoon salt. Give them a stir and cook until everything is combined and warmed through, about 1 minute.

5. Spoon the spinach mixture onto a serving platter and top with the scallops. Serve family-style.

1 pound large scallops

1½ teaspoons fine sea salt

1 teaspoon smoked paprika

½ teaspoon freshly cracked black pepper

3 tablespoons salted butter

3 tablespoons extra-virgin olive oil

3 tablespoons unfiltered apple cider vinegar

¼ cup golden raisins

4 garlic cloves, thinly sliced

1 bunch spinach (about ½ pound)

1 tablespoon maple syrup

Serves 4

Prep Time: 20 Minutes

Cook Time: 30 Minutes

Gluten-Free

Kid-Friendly

SALMON WITH FRIED SHALLOT MASHED POTATOES

An old-school meat-and-potatoes dinner this is not! Studded with fried shallots and seasoned with garlic, the mashed potatoes are not the glue-like butter bombs of old. Speaking of mashed potatoes, this recipe will serve four very, very hungry people or you might end up with some leftovers. Either add another half pound of salmon to serve six people, or just liberally taste-test along the way.

½ cup vegetable oil

¾ pound shallots, thinly sliced (about 5 medium)

3½ teaspoons fine sea salt

1 bunch baby broccoli (about ½ pound)

3 pounds russet potatoes, peeled and cut into 2-inch cubes

4 (4-ounce) skin-on salmon fillets

¼ teaspoon freshly cracked black pepper

1 cup (2 sticks) unsalted butter, softened

½ cup whole milk

½ teaspoon garlic powder

1. Preheat the oven to 425°F with a rack in the center position. Line a rimmed sheet pan with parchment paper.

2. Heat the vegetable oil in a large skillet over medium-high heat. Once the oil is glistening, add the shallots and cook, stirring often, until golden brown, 7 to 10 minutes. Using a slotted spoon, transfer the shallots to a paper towel–lined plate. Reserve the oil in the pan.

3. Meanwhile, fill a large pot with 4 quarts water and season with 2 teaspoons of the salt. Bring to a boil over high heat. Add the baby broccoli and cook until bright green, about 2 minutes. Using a slotted spoon or tongs, transfer the baby broccoli to the prepared sheet pan and pat dry. Reserve the water in the pot.

4. Add the potatoes to the reserved hot water over high heat and return to a boil. Cook until just fork tender, about 15 minutes. Drain.

5. Meanwhile, add the salmon skin side down to the sheet pan with the baby broccoli. Drizzle the reserved shallot oil all over the salmon and baby broccoli and season with ¾ teaspoon of the salt and the pepper. Bake for 10 to 12 minutes, until the salmon easily flakes with a fork and the baby broccoli is browned on the bottom.

6. In the pot used to cook the potatoes, combine the butter and milk over medium-low heat. Cook, stirring, until the butter is melted, about 2 minutes. Using a potato ricer, rice the potatoes over the hot butter mixture. (Alternatively, mash the potatoes directly into the liquid, taking care not to overwork them.) Season with the garlic powder and the remaining ¾ teaspoon salt. Stir in about three quarters of the shallots. Adjust the seasoning to taste.

7. To serve, spoon the potatoes into bowls and add a piece of salmon and some baby broccoli on top. Top with the remaining shallots, dividing evenly.

NOT YOUR MOTHER'S TUNA CASSEROLE

Serves 8
Prep Time: 15 Minutes
Cook Time: 50 Minutes

We've got a real soft spot for retro food. But often when it comes to actually cooking the dishes we remember so fondly, it turns out the nostalgic recipes are best left in the past. That doesn't mean you can't take the concept, make some smart ingredient swaps, and give the whole thing an upgrade! Here, we've given classic tuna casserole a serious makeover. No canned soup, potato chips, or water-packed tuna here. Instead, oil-packed tuna partners up with punchy Parmesan and nutty Gruyère to make for a thoroughly modern tuna casserole.

1. Preheat the oven to 425°F with a rack in the center position. Grease a 9 x 13-inch baking dish with olive oil.

2. Heat 2 tablespoons of the oil in a large skillet over medium heat. Once the oil is glistening, add the leeks and cook, stirring occasionally, until softened, about 4 minutes. Add the garlic and cook until fragrant, about 1 more minute. Transfer to the prepared baking dish. Add the cabbage and tuna and toss to combine.

3. To the same skillet, add the heavy cream, Gruyère, ¼ cup of the Parmesan, the thyme, salt, pepper, and nutmeg. Bring to a simmer over medium-high heat and cook, stirring continuously, until the cheese melts and the sauce thickens slightly, about 5 minutes. Pour the sauce over the cabbage mixture and toss to coat. Smooth into an even layer and bake for 30 minutes.

4. Meanwhile, in a small bowl, combine the panko with the remaining ¼ cup Parmesan and the remaining 3 tablespoons oil. Stir to mix well.

5. Remove the baking dish from the oven, scatter the panko mixture over the top, and return to the oven. Continue baking until the panko is golden brown, another 7 to 8 minutes.

6. Let the casserole sit for 5 minutes before serving.

5 tablespoons extra-virgin olive oil, plus more for greasing

3 cups trimmed and thinly sliced leeks (from 3 large leeks) (see Note)

4 garlic cloves, minced

5 cups shredded green cabbage (about 1 pound)

2 (5-ounce) cans oil-packed tuna, drained

2 cups heavy cream

4 ounces Gruyère cheese, grated

½ cup freshly grated Parmesan cheese

2 teaspoons fresh thyme leaves

1 teaspoon kosher salt

½ teaspoon freshly cracked black pepper

¼ teaspoon ground nutmeg

1 cup panko breadcrumbs

Note: If you've never worked with leeks, there are a few things to know first. Despite being gloriously tall, those dark green tops are not edible—you want to slice them off and discard them, in addition to trimming the root. The remaining white and light green parts can be tricky to clean since the tightly bound rings tend to trap dirt. Halve lengthwise, then fan out the layers under running water to rinse it all away. Now slice, cook, and enjoy!

Serves 4

Prep Time: 15 Minutes

Cook Time: 30 Minutes

SHRIMP EN PAPILLOTE WITH COUSCOUS SALAD

Wait, stop—come back! We know, you see a phrase like "en papillote" and you're like, "On to the next one!" But all en papillote means is "in parchment paper," and it's a very, very simple way of cooking. You might have parchment paper around for baking, but get ready to use it at dinnertime, too. Essentially, baking en papillote steams whatever is inside the little envelope you create, and it's a near-foolproof way to ensure tender, moist meat. The method is especially lovely for cooking seafood, which always benefits from a delicate touch. Here, fresh lemon infuses your pouches of shrimp and garlicky couscous with its citrusy aroma so when you pop them open at the table and the fragrant steam fills the air, everyone will be in love with dinner even before they've had their first bite. No one has to know how incredibly easy this impressive and crowd-pleasing meal was to pull off. Your secret is safe with us.

1½ cups chicken stock

1 cup dried pearl couscous, rinsed

1 tablespoon extra-virgin olive oil

1½ teaspoons kosher salt

½ teaspoon garlic powder

1½ cups snap peas, halved horizontally

1 small shallot, minced

¼ cup finely chopped fresh flat-leaf parsley leaves, plus more for garnish

1 tablespoon fresh lemon juice (from 1 lemon) plus 1 lemon, thinly sliced

1 pound large raw tail-on shrimp, peeled and deveined

2 tablespoons salted butter

Freshly cracked black pepper

1. Preheat the oven 375°F with a rack in the center position. Cut parchment paper into four 15 x 10-inch ovals. Fold in half crosswise.

2. In a medium pot over high heat, bring the chicken stock to a rapid boil. Add the couscous, olive oil, 1 teaspoon of the salt, and the garlic powder. Reduce to a simmer, cover, and cook until all the liquid has been absorbed, about 10 minutes. Remove the pot from the heat and stir in the snap peas, shallot, parsley, and lemon juice.

3. Unfold the parchment sheets. On one half of each sheet, layer on the couscous, lemon slices, and shrimp, dividing evenly. Sprinkle the remaining ½ teaspoon salt over the shrimp. Top each packet with ½ tablespoon butter.

4. Close the parchment by refolding it over the prepared shrimp and carefully roll the edges toward the center to seal. Arrange the pouches on a rimmed sheet pan. Bake for 18 minutes.

5. Transfer the pouches to individual plates. Using a fork, unroll the edges of the parchment, then carefully open the pouches to release the steam and expose the contents. Top with additional parsley and black pepper to serve.

COCONUT SHRIMP WITH PEANUT NOODLES

Serves 6
Prep Time: 30 Minutes
Cook Time: 15 Minutes
Dairy-Free
Kid-Friendly

This dish is made of two recipes that are delicious on their own, but that we happen to love to eat together. The savory-sweet, crunchy coated shrimp are the perfect hit of both flavor and texture atop the salty, smooth sauce-slathered noodles. That sauce is what ties this dish together—and we're certain you'll want more for dipping on the side. You could make these two things separately for a wonderful appetizer or an easy lunch, but when you combine them, you have a hearty dinner that hits pretty much every note.

1. Preheat the oven to 425°F with a rack in the center position. Line a rimmed sheet pan with parchment paper.

2. Bring a large pot of water to a boil over high heat. Cook the noodles according to the package instructions. Drain and transfer to a serving bowl.

3. Meanwhile, in a shallow bowl, stir together the almond flour, paprika, onion powder, garlic powder, salt, and pepper. In a second shallow bowl, beat the eggs. In a third shallow bowl, place ¾ cup of the shredded coconut. (See Note.)

4. Working with one piece at a time, dip the shrimp into the flour mixture and turn to coat. Then dip it into the egg, letting the excess drip off. Then dip it into the coconut, gently pressing to adhere. Arrange the coated shrimp on the prepared sheet pan as they're finished. Add more coconut to the bowl, ¾ cup at a time to prevent clumping, as needed.

5. Bake for 12 minutes, or until the shrimp are pink and the coconut is beginning to brown on the edges.

6. Stir half of the peanut sauce into the noodles. Top with the shrimp, cilantro, and crushed peanuts. Serve with the remaining peanut sauce alongside for dipping.

3 (3-ounce) packages ramen, seasoning packets discarded

1 cup almond flour

1 teaspoon paprika

1 teaspoon onion powder

1 teaspoon garlic powder

1 teaspoon fine sea salt

¼ teaspoon freshly cracked black pepper

4 large eggs

3 cups shredded sweetened coconut

1¼ pounds large, raw tail-on shrimp, peeled and deveined

1 recipe Peanut Sauce (page 275), warmed

Fresh cilantro leaves, for serving

Crushed peanuts, for serving

Note: We use shallow bowls for dredging because they're easy to get ingredients in and out of—there's a good amount of surface area. Pie dishes or cake pans work great, too!

Serves 4
Prep Time: 15 Minutes
Cook Time: 20 Minutes
<35 Minutes
Dairy-Free
Gluten-Free

NIÇOISE SALAD

Our version of this summery composed salad—which is perhaps the iconic dish of the French Riviera—is built around good-quality, oil-packed tinned fish. But don't let a fish aversion keep you from trying this recipe! It can easily be adapted: If you're vegetarian, try chickpeas or white beans in place of fish. If you're a carnivore, sliced, grilled steak makes a great swap. With salty make-everything-taste-better bursts like capers and olives speckled throughout this beautiful platter of freshness, there's plenty of room for play. You can even switch up the vegetables depending on what's in season or on hand—try adding snap peas, radishes, shaved carrots, or even sliced bell peppers. We encourage you to make this dish your own! It will be great no matter what you choose.

2 teaspoons fine sea salt

6 ounces green beans, trimmed

¾ pound new potatoes, halved

4 cups roughly chopped butter lettuce

¼ cup fresh basil leaves

½ cup Honey Mustard Vinaigrette (page 272)

12 ounces oil-packed tinned fish, such as smoked trout or tuna, drained

½ cup Kalamata olives, pitted and drained

¼ cup capers, drained

1 cup cherry tomatoes, halved

3 Persian cucumbers, sliced

Freshly cracked black pepper

Flaky salt

1. Fill a large bowl with ice water.

2. Fill a large pot with 6 quarts water and add the fine salt. Bring to a boil over high heat. Add the green beans and cook until bright green, 2 to 3 minutes. Using tongs, transfer the green beans to the ice water to stop cooking, reserving the boiling water in the pot.

3. To the boiling water, add the potatoes and cook until just tender, 12 to 15 minutes. Drain and transfer to the ice water. Let cool in the water for 1 to 2 minutes. Transfer to a plate and pat the green beans and potatoes dry.

4. In a large bowl, combine the lettuce and basil with half of the dressing. Toss to coat. Arrange on a serving platter. Top with the green beans, potatoes, fish, olives, capers, tomatoes, and cucumbers.

5. Drizzle the remaining dressing over the top. Season to taste with black pepper and flaky salt before serving.

SALMON AND JOJOS
WITH TARTAR SAUCE

Serves 4
Prep Time: 20 Minutes
Cook Time: 30 Minutes
Dairy-Free
Kid-Friendly
Sheet Pan

Jojos, for the uninitiated, are what we Pacific Northwesterners (and Midwesterners, too, for that matter) call seasoned, fried potato wedges. Holly grew up getting them as a treat on road trips, grabbing them at gas stations along the way. Now they're a beloved dive bar snack. Here, we've paired them with salmon—yet another classic PNW ingredient—to make our own spin on fish and chips. A crunchy crust, spot-on spice mix, lots of fresh dill, and the perfect dipping sauce make this a fresh take worthy of much more than a car ride. No messy deep-frying necessary.

1. **Make the jojos.** Preheat the oven to 450°F. Line a rimmed sheet pan with parchment paper.

2. In a small bowl, stir together the brown sugar, celery salt, garlic powder, pepper, and paprika. Place the potatoes on the prepared sheet pan and drizzle them with the olive oil. Sprinkle the spice mixture over the potatoes and toss to coat. Bake for 15 minutes.

3. **Meanwhile, make the salmon.** In a shallow bowl, stir together the flour, celery salt, garlic powder, pepper, and paprika. In a second shallow bowl, beat the eggs. In a third shallow bowl, combine the panko and plain breadcrumbs. (See Note on page 203.)

4. Pat the salmon dry and sprinkle with the salt. Dip each piece of salmon into the flour mixture, turning to coat. Next dip the salmon in the eggs, allowing the excess to drip off. Then dip the salmon into the panko mixture, gently pressing to adhere.

5. Once the potatoes have baked for 15 minutes, remove the sheet pan from the oven. Add the dredged salmon in between the potatoes. Mist the salmon with cooking spray. Return the sheet pan to the oven and bake until the potatoes and salmon are both golden brown, about 15 more minutes.

6. **Meanwhile, make the tartar sauce.** In a small bowl, stir together the mayonnaise, pickles, capers, Dijon, celery salt, paprika, and garlic powder.

7. Sprinkle the salmon and potatoes with fresh dill, a squeeze of lemon juice, and flaky salt. Serve with the tartar sauce alongside.

JOJOS

2 teaspoons light brown sugar

1 teaspoon celery salt

1 teaspoon garlic powder

¼ teaspoon freshly cracked black pepper

½ teaspoon paprika

2 large russet potatoes (about 1½ pounds), scrubbed and cut into 1½-inch-thick wedges

3 tablespoons extra-virgin olive oil

SALMON

½ cup all-purpose flour

1 teaspoon celery salt

1 teaspoon garlic powder

¼ teaspoon freshly cracked black pepper

½ teaspoon paprika

2 large eggs

½ cup panko breadcrumbs

½ cup plain breadcrumbs

1 to 1¼ pounds salmon, skin removed and cut into 1-inch strips

1 teaspoon kosher salt

Cooking spray

TARTAR SAUCE

½ cup mayonnaise

¼ cup minced dill pickles

1 tablespoon minced capers

1 teaspoon Dijon mustard

¼ teaspoon celery salt

¼ teaspoon paprika

¼ teaspoon garlic powder

Minced fresh dill, for serving

Lemon wedges, for serving

Flaky salt, for serving

Serves 6

Prep Time: 10 Minutes

Cook Time: 30 Minutes

Dairy-Free

Kid-Friendly

SEAFOOD PAELLA-ISH

We love eating paella. Making it, however, not so much. It's tricky and time-consuming to get the rice cooked just so, and we're not always (or ever) up for the open-flame cooking situation it traditionally requires. What's rice-like but much easier to work with? Orzo! The lovely little pasta stands in here, cooking so much faster while still absorbing all of the smoky, tomato-rich flavors that we crave in paella. The rest of the dish is adaptable, too. If you can't find mussels, use clams. Or if you're not into seafood at all, try this recipe with shredded chicken—it'll still be fantastic.

1 tablespoon extra-virgin olive oil

1 small yellow onion, finely chopped

1 large red bell pepper, cut into ½-inch-thick strips

2 garlic cloves, minced

1 quart chicken stock

1 (14-ounce) can fire-roasted diced tomatoes, drained

2 cups orzo

2 teaspoons smoked paprika

¾ teaspoon fine sea salt

1 cup fresh or frozen peas

¼ cup minced fresh flat-leaf parsley leaves, plus more for serving

1 pound large raw tail-on shrimp, peeled and deveined

1 pound mussels or clams

Lemon wedges, for serving

1. Heat the olive oil in a large skillet or braiser over medium heat. Once the oil is glistening, add the onion and bell pepper and cook, stirring occasionally, until the onion is softened and translucent, 5 to 7 minutes. Add the garlic and cook until fragrant, about 1 more minute.

2. Add the stock, tomatoes, orzo, 1 cup water, the paprika, and the salt. Bring to a boil over medium-high heat and cook, stirring often, until most of the liquid has been absorbed, about 10 minutes. Stir in the peas and parsley. Arrange the shrimp and mussels in an even layer over the top. Reduce the heat to low, cover, and cook until the shrimp is opaque and the mussels have opened, about 10 more minutes.

3. Squeeze lemon juice over the entire dish and garnish with more parsley. Serve family-style.

MEATBALLS

Serves 8

Prep Time: 10 Minutes

Cook Time: 1 Hour 10 Minutes

Kid-Friendly

SPAGHETTI AND MEATBALLS

Herby, rich meatballs simmered in the simplest homemade tomato sauce—that's all anyone really wants, right? We have a few tricks for making these meatballs transcendently delicious. First of all, when you're mixing the meat, use your hands and try to have a light touch. Overmixing is the enemy of a tender meatball. Second, a nice slow simmer in a tomato sauce inspired by the ultimate doyenne of Italian cookery, Marcella Hazan, allows them to release their flavors over time. While we don't claim to be actual Italian *nonnas*, one thing we know the nonnas would approve of: It'll feed a big crowd—and then some. If you're not cooking for your whole extended family and all the cousins, you can always halve the recipe, or do your future self a solid and freeze half of the meatballs and sauce for another day.

3 (28-ounce) cans whole stewed tomatoes

2 (28-ounce) cans tomato sauce

3 large white onions, halved

1 cup (2 sticks) salted butter

2 pounds 80/20 ground beef

1 pound ground pork

3 large eggs

1 cup Italian-style breadcrumbs

¾ cup finely chopped fresh flat-leaf parsley leaves, plus more for serving

5 ounces freshly grated Parmesan cheese, plus more for serving

6 garlic cloves, minced

1 tablespoon kosher salt

2 teaspoons freshly cracked black pepper

2 pounds cooked spaghetti, for serving

Note: If you prefer a smoother sauce, you can hit yours with an immersion blender after you remove the onions.

1. In a large pot, combine the whole tomatoes and their juices, crushing the tomatoes a bit with your hands as you add them; the tomato sauce; the onions; and the butter. Bring to a boil over medium-high heat, then reduce the heat to a simmer. Cook, stirring often, until the onions are softened, about 40 minutes. Using tongs, carefully discard the onions.

2. While the sauce is simmering, make the meatballs. In a large bowl, combine the beef, pork, eggs, breadcrumbs, parsley, Parmesan, garlic, salt, and pepper. Mix well, then with wet hands, form golf ball–size balls (about 2 tablespoons each). You should have 40 to 45 meatballs.

3. Carefully add the meatballs to the sauce. Return the sauce to a simmer over medium heat, then reduce the heat to low, cover, and cook for 30 minutes, or until the meatballs are cooked through.

4. Serve the meatballs and tomato sauce over spaghetti topped with additional parsley and Parmesan.

MISO GINGER MEATBALLS WITH CABBAGE

Serves 6
Prep Time: 20 Minutes
Cook Time: 20 Minutes
Dairy-Free
Kid-Friendly

Loaded with miso, carrot, ginger, and garlic, these meatballs are the perfect meal if you're looking for a fresh and lively take. And while they're delicious, they aren't really the star here—that spotlight is saved for cabbage. Cabbage is way more than coleslaw filler or an overcooked side for corned beef. Pan-frying it over high heat maintains the integrity of its crunch, but warms it up just enough to soak in the miso sauce we've whipped up to go with it.

1. In a large bowl, stir together the eggs and 1 tablespoon of the miso paste until fully incorporated. Add the pork, panko, carrot, minced green onions, garlic, ginger, salt, and pepper. Mix well, then with wet hands, form golf ball–size meatballs (about 2 tablespoons each) and place on a sheet pan. You should have about 20 meatballs.

2. Heat 1 tablespoon of the sesame oil in a large skillet over high heat. Once the oil is smoking, add the cabbage and sliced green onions. Cook, stirring often, until the cabbage begins to brown slightly, about 2 minutes. Transfer the cabbage and green onions to a plate.

3. Reduce the heat to medium and add the remaining 1½ tablespoons sesame oil. Once the oil is glistening, add the meatballs in a single layer. Cook, undisturbed, until the meatballs are just browned on the bottom, 2 to 3 minutes. Turn them carefully and cook to brown the opposite side, 2 to 3 more minutes.

4. In a small bowl, stir together the coconut aminos and the remaining 1 tablespoon miso paste until fully incorporated. Pour the sauce over the meatballs in the skillet and turn to coat. Bring the sauce to a simmer. Cover and continue cooking until the meatballs are cooked through, about 5 more minutes. Return the cabbage and green onions to the skillet and toss to combine.

5. Serve the dish as is, or spoon it over rice and top with sesame seeds, if desired.

2 large eggs

2 tablespoons yellow miso paste

1½ pounds ground pork

1 cup panko breadcrumbs

¼ cup peeled and grated carrot

¼ cup minced green onion (white and green parts) plus 4 whole green onions cut into 3-inch pieces (1 bunch total)

4 garlic cloves, minced

1 tablespoon minced peeled fresh ginger

1½ teaspoons kosher salt

¼ teaspoon freshly cracked black pepper

2½ tablespoons sesame oil

4 cups roughly torn green cabbage (about 12 ounces)

¼ cup coconut aminos (see Note on page 156)

Cooked rice, for serving (optional)

Sesame seeds, for serving (optional)

Serves 4
Prep Time: 30 Minutes
Cook Time: 30 Minutes
Kid-Friendly

PAPRIKA CHICKEN MEATBALLS IN TOMATO SAUCE WITH LEMON DILL CREAM

If there's even a hint of a chance that the defining flavors of any dish can be reworked in the form of a meatball, we've tried it. Some recipes are more successful than others, admittedly, and these paprikash-inspired meatballs are one of our greatest hits. Sweet Hungarian paprika sets the tone for this brick-hued dish, while other classic Central European ingredients, like dill, lemon, and sour cream, bring a crisp, contrasting lift in the form of a creamy sauce served on the side for dolloping and dipping.

LEMON DILL CREAM

½ cup sour cream

2 teaspoons minced fresh dill

1 teaspoon grated lemon zest

1 tablespoon fresh lemon juice (from 1 lemon)

¼ teaspoon kosher salt

¼ teaspoon cayenne pepper

MEATBALLS

1 pound ground chicken

¼ cup plain breadcrumbs

1 large egg

2 garlic cloves, grated

1¼ teaspoons kosher salt

1 teaspoon grated lemon zest

1 teaspoon paprika

1 teaspoon minced fresh dill

¼ teaspoon freshly cracked black pepper

2 tablespoons extra-virgin olive oil

TOMATO SAUCE

1 medium yellow onion, chopped

2 garlic cloves, minced

1 (14-ounce) can crushed tomatoes

1 cup chicken stock

1 tablespoon paprika

1 teaspoon kosher salt

1 teaspoon caraway seeds

Lemon wedges, for serving

Minced fresh flat-leaf parsley leaves, for serving

1. **Make the lemon dill cream.** In a small bowl, combine the sour cream, dill, lemon zest and juice, salt, and cayenne. Stir to mix well.

2. **Make the meatballs.** In a large bowl, combine the chicken, breadcrumbs, egg, garlic, salt, lemon zest, paprika, dill, and pepper. Mix well, then with wet hands, form golf ball–size meatballs (about 2 tablespoons each) and place on a plate. You should have about 15 meatballs.

3. Heat the olive oil in a large nonstick skillet over medium-high heat. Once the oil is glistening, add the meatballs in a single layer. Cook, undisturbed, until the meatballs are just browned on the bottom, about 3 minutes. Turn them carefully and cook to brown the opposite side, about 3 more minutes. Transfer the meatballs to a plate, leaving the oil behind in the skillet.

4. **Make the sauce.** Add the onion to the same skillet over medium heat and cook, stirring occasionally, until softened and translucent, about 5 minutes. Add the garlic and cook until fragrant, about 1 more minute. Add the tomatoes, chicken stock, paprika, salt, and caraway. Use an immersion blender to blend the sauce directly in the skillet. (Alternatively, transfer the onion, garlic, and oil to the base of a blender. Add the tomatoes, chicken stock, paprika, salt, and caraway and blend on high until smooth, about 2 minutes. Then return the sauce to the skillet.)

5. Return the meatballs to the skillet and bring to a simmer over medium heat. Cover and cook until the meatballs are cooked through, about 10 minutes.

6. Transfer the meatballs and sauce to a serving dish and dollop the lemon dill cream over the top. Serve with a squeeze of lemon juice and a sprinkle of parsley.

POTLUCK-STYLE TERIYAKI MEATBALLS AND MACARONI SALAD

Serves: 8
Prep Time: 15 Minutes
Cook Time: 30 Minutes
Dairy-Free
Kid-Friendly

If potlucks were a part of your life when you were growing up, this recipe might look familiar. We both have nostalgic memories of long Sunday afternoons spent around a table weighed down with Crock-Pots full of goodies and tub after tub of mayo-slicked salads. You could almost always count on finding tiny teriyaki meatballs and macaroni salad, purchased from the store by the gallon. We still crave those familiar flavors, and thanks to these upgraded versions—pasta salad from scratch, please!—we can once again confidently vouch for them as very legit party food. With so many powerful ingredients at work, you might be tempted to think the curry powder is overkill, but it's the secret ingredient—in both the meatballs and the macaroni—that ties everything together.

1. Preheat the oven to 375°F. Line a rimmed sheet pan with parchment paper.

2. **Make the teriyaki sauce.** In a small bowl, stir the cornstarch into 1 cup water. In a small saucepan, whisk together the brown sugar, soy sauce, honey, ginger, and garlic powder. Stir in the cornstarch mixture. Bring the sauce to a simmer over medium-high heat. Reduce the heat to medium-low and cook until it reaches your desired thickness, 3 to 5 minutes. Remove and let cool slightly.

3. **Make the meatballs.** In a large bowl, combine the turkey, breadcrumbs, onion, eggs, garlic, ¼ cup of the teriyaki sauce, the curry powder, and the salt. Mix well, then with wet hands, form meatballs (about 1½ tablespoons each) and place on the prepared sheet pan. You should have about 30 meatballs. Bake for 14 to 16 minutes, or until cooked through.

4. **Meanwhile, make the macaroni salad.** Fill a large pot with 4 quarts water and add 2 teaspoons of the salt. Bring to a boil over high heat. Add the pasta and cook to al dente according to the package directions. Drain well and rinse with cold water.

5. In a large serving bowl, whisk together the mayonnaise, ¼ cup of the teriyaki sauce, the vinegar, onion powder, yellow curry powder, the remaining ½ teaspoon salt, and the pepper. Add the pasta, carrots, and green onions and toss to combine. Cover and refrigerate until ready to serve.

6. Place the meatballs in a large serving bowl. Add the remaining teriyaki sauce and toss to coat. Serve with the macaroni salad alongside.

TERIYAKI SAUCE
1½ tablespoons cornstarch

½ cup light brown sugar

⅓ cup low-sodium soy sauce or tamari

1 tablespoon honey

¼ teaspoon ground ginger

¼ teaspoon garlic powder

MEATBALLS
2 pounds ground turkey

½ cup plain breadcrumbs

1 medium yellow onion, grated, liquid drained (see Note)

2 large eggs

6 garlic cloves, minced

2 teaspoons yellow curry powder

2 teaspoons kosher salt

MACARONI SALAD
2½ teaspoons kosher salt

¾ pound elbow macaroni

1 cup mayonnaise

1 teaspoon unfiltered apple cider vinegar

1 teaspoon onion powder

½ teaspoon yellow curry powder

¼ teaspoon freshly cracked black pepper

⅓ cup peeled and grated carrots

5 green onions, white and green parts, finely chopped

Note: Ever heard the term "sweat an onion"? They're full of liquid! We call for grating it here, which is going to release all that water, so you'll want to drain it, too. Two choices: Either place the grated onion in a clean kitchen towel and wring it out, or place the onion in a fine-mesh sieve and press down with a spatula.

Serves 6
Prep Time: 15 Minutes
Cook Time: 25 Minutes
Kid-Friendly
Sheet Pan

MEATBALLS

2 pounds ground chicken

1 cup panko breadcrumbs

3 large eggs

½ small red onion, grated, liquid drained (see Note on page 219)

¼ cup minced fresh flat-leaf parsley leaves

4 garlic cloves, minced

2 teaspoons fresh lemon juice (from ½ lemon)

2 teaspoons kosher salt

2 teaspoons dried oregano

1 teaspoon minced fresh rosemary

Extra-virgin olive oil

TZATZIKI

1 cup plain Greek yogurt

1 cup grated cucumber (from 1 English cucumber)

2 tablespoons fresh lemon juice (from 1 lemon)

1 tablespoon dried dill

1 teaspoon minced garlic

½ teaspoon fine sea salt

¼ teaspoon freshly cracked black pepper

FOR SERVING
Pita

Sliced tomato

Sliced cucumber

Sliced red onion

Pitted Kalamata olives

BAKED CHICKEN SOUVLAKI MEATBALL WRAP

Souvlaki hails from Greece and is easily one of our favorite street foods, right up there with doner kebabs and gyros, some of its Mediterranean relatives. Brightly seasoned, skewered meat, usually served in pita, souvlaki can be made with lamb or pork but is often made with good old chicken breast. We've lifted the beautiful Greek flavors we love—fresh lemon, oregano, parsley, and garlic—and applied them to one of our favorite meaty mediums: chicken meatballs! They make an irresistible wrap, but don't feel confined to serving them that way. For a lighter meal, place them over a green salad, or simply snack on them! However you eat them, promise us you won't skip the tzatziki. It's ready in just a couple minutes, and it really makes the meatballs shine.

1. Preheat the oven to 400°F. Line a rimmed sheet pan with parchment paper.

2. **Make the meatballs.** In a large bowl, combine the chicken, breadcrumbs, eggs, red onion, parsley, garlic, lemon juice, kosher salt, oregano, and rosemary. Mix well, then with wet hands, form golf ball–size meatballs (about 2 tablespoons each) and place on the prepared sheet pan. You should have about 20 meatballs.

3. Brush the meatballs with olive oil and bake for 20 minutes, or until just cooked through. Brush the meatballs with oil again and turn the oven to broil. Broil until the meatballs are golden brown, 3 to 4 minutes.

4. **Meanwhile, make the tzatziki.** In a small bowl, stir together the yogurt, cucumber, lemon juice, dill, garlic, fine salt, and pepper.

5. Serve the meatballs wrapped in pita bread topped with tzatziki, tomato, cucumber, red onion, and olives.

SWEET AND SPICY
CHICKEN MEATBALLS

Serves 4
Prep Time: 10 Minutes
Cook Time: 25 Minutes
<35 Minutes
Dairy-Free
Kid-Friendly

A double dose of garlic and fresh green onions gives these chicken meatballs plenty of punch, while a little chili sauce brings a hint of heat. Their sweetness comes from the slightly sticky sauce they cook in, and it's a great foil for that chili kick. While these meatballs can easily be dinner—serve them over rice and call it a day—we love them as party food, too. Pop them on a platter with some toothpicks for stabbing and a little bowl of whatever's left of the sauce on the side for dipping.

1. Make the meatballs. In a medium bowl, combine the chicken, panko, green onions, egg, chili garlic sauce, sesame oil, salt, and garlic powder. Mix well, then with wet hands, form golf ball–size meatballs (about 2 tablespoons each) and place on a plate. You should have about 16 meatballs.

2. Heat the vegetable oil in a large skillet over medium heat. Once the oil is glistening, add the meatballs in a single layer. Cook, undisturbed, until the meatballs are just browned on the bottom, about 3 minutes. Turn them carefully and cook to brown the opposite side, about 3 minutes.

3. Meanwhile, make the sauce. In a medium bowl, whisk together the brown sugar, chili garlic sauce, soy sauce, vinegar, and sesame oil. In a separate small bowl, whisk the cornstarch into 1 cup water until dissolved, then whisk the mixture into the sauce until smooth.

4. Once the meatballs are browned, pour the sauce into the pan to cover them. Bring the sauce to a simmer, stir to incorporate and coat the meatballs, 1 to 2 minutes. Then cover the pan and cook until the meatballs are cooked through, 8 to 10 minutes.

5. Using a slotted spoon, transfer the meatballs to a serving platter. Sprinkle them with sesame seeds and more green onions. Pour the sauce into a small bowl and serve alongside the meatballs.

MEATBALLS
1 pound ground chicken
⅔ cup panko breadcrumbs
3 green onions, white and green parts, finely chopped (about ¼ cup), plus more for serving
1 large egg
2 teaspoons chili garlic sauce
1 teaspoon toasted sesame oil
1 teaspoon kosher salt
½ teaspoon garlic powder
2 tablespoons vegetable oil
Sesame seeds, for serving

SAUCE
1 cup packed light brown sugar
1 tablespoon chili garlic sauce
¼ cup soy sauce or tamari
2 tablespoons rice vinegar
2 teaspoons toasted sesame oil
1½ tablespoons cornstarch

Serves 6
Prep Time: 15 Minutes
Cook Time: 30 Minutes
Kid-Friendly

SPICED LAMB MEATBALLS WITH CILANTRO YOGURT

Fragrant and colorful, this stunning one-pot supper is a feast fit for royalty. Or at least for your most difficult-to-surprise food-loving friends. We use a generous hand to season these meatballs, and to really let those warm, wonderful spices sing, we temper the ground lamb's powerful meatiness with a bit of beef. The meatballs and sunshine-hued turmeric rice steam together in one pot, making for easy prep and painless cleanup. Cooling cilantro yogurt ties the whole dish together with its refreshingly tangy, herby brightness.

MEATBALLS AND RICE

1 pound ground lamb

½ pound 80/20 ground beef

2 large eggs

½ cup panko breadcrumbs

¼ cup finely chopped fresh cilantro

4 garlic cloves, minced

1½ teaspoons garam masala

2 teaspoons kosher salt

1 teaspoon ground cinnamon

½ teaspoon minced peeled fresh ginger

3 tablespoons extra-virgin olive oil

2 cups basmati rice, rinsed and drained

1 teaspoon ground turmeric

CILANTRO YOGURT

1 cup plain Greek yogurt

¼ cup finely chopped fresh cilantro, plus more for garnish

2 garlic cloves, minced

3 tablespoons fresh lemon juice (from 1 to 2 lemons)

1 tablespoon extra-virgin olive oil

1 teaspoon garam masala

1 teaspoon kosher salt

1. Make the meatballs and rice. In a large bowl, combine the lamb, beef, eggs, panko, cilantro, garlic, 1 teaspoon of the garam masala, 1 teaspoon of the salt, ½ teaspoon of the cinnamon, and the ginger. Mix well, then with wet hands, form golf ball–size meatballs (about 2 tablespoons each) and place on a plate. You should have about 18 meatballs.

2. Heat 1 tablespoon of the olive oil in a large pot over medium heat. Once the oil is glistening, working in batches, add the meatballs in a single layer. Cook, undisturbed, until the meatballs are just browned on the bottom, 2 to 3 minutes. Turn them carefully and cook to brown the opposite side, 2 to 3 minutes. Transfer the meatballs back to the plate.

3. Add the remaining 2 tablespoons olive oil over medium heat. Once the oil is glistening, add the rice, turmeric, the remaining 1 teaspoon salt, the remaining ½ teaspoon garam masala, and the remaining ½ teaspoon cinnamon. Cook, stirring, until the rice is opaque and the spices are fragrant, about 4 minutes. Add 3 cups water and stir to combine. Increase the heat to high and bring to a boil, then return the browned meatballs and any collected juices to the pot. Reduce the heat to low, cover, and cook until the liquid has been absorbed, the rice is tender, and the meatballs are cooked through, about 20 minutes.

4. Meanwhile, make the cilantro yogurt. In a medium bowl, stir together the yogurt, cilantro, garlic, lemon juice, olive oil, garam masala, and salt.

5. Serve the meatballs with more cilantro to garnish and with the cilantro yogurt alongside.

PORK MEATBALL BOWL WITH MOJO SAUCE

Serves 4
Prep Time: 20 Minutes
Cook Time: 35 Minutes
Dairy-Free
Gluten-Free
Kid-Friendly

If you've never tasted Cuban mojo sauce, you're in for a major treat. Traditionally made with lots of garlic, sour orange juice, olive oil, and sometimes chilies, it's one of our favorites. Sour oranges are not so easy to come by here in the United States, so this version emulates their unique punch with a combo of lime and regular orange juices. Parsley and cilantro make the sauce bright green—a feast for the eyes that preps your palate for the flavor explosion to come. Simple pork meatballs, succulent and ready for a perk-up, are the ideal vehicle for this zesty sauce. While they bake, fry up some plantains, warm some beans, and get ready to tuck into a meal as colorful and vibrant as the culture it pays homage to.

1. **Make the sauce.** In the base of a blender or food processor, combine the cilantro, parsley, garlic, jalapeño, olive oil, orange zest and juice, lime juice, honey, salt, cumin, and oregano. Blend until almost smooth, scraping down the sides as needed, about 3 minutes.

2. **Make the meatballs.** Preheat the oven to 400°F. Line a rimmed sheet pan with parchment paper.

3. In a large bowl, combine the pork, eggs, breadcrumbs, 2 tablespoons of the mojo sauce, 1 teaspoon salt, and the pepper. Mix well, then with wet hands, form golf ball–size meatballs (about 2 tablespoons each) and place on the prepared sheet pan. You should have about 13 meatballs. Bake for 20 minutes, or until the meatballs are cooked through.

4. Meanwhile, heat the vegetable oil in a large skillet over medium-high heat. Once the oil is glistening, add the plantains and cook until golden brown, 2 to 3 minutes per side. Using tongs, transfer the plantains to a paper towel–lined plate, leaving the oil behind, and immediately season with salt to taste.

5. In the same skillet over medium heat, add the onion. Cook, stirring occasionally, until softened and translucent, about 5 minutes. Stir in the black beans and cook until warmed through, about 3 minutes. Season with salt to taste.

6. To serve, divide the rice, beans, onion, plantains, and meatballs among 4 bowls. Drizzle the remaining mojo sauce over the top and garnish with cilantro.

MOJO SAUCE

1 cup loosely packed fresh cilantro, plus fresh leaves for serving

½ cup loosely packed fresh flat-leaf parsley leaves

4 garlic cloves

1 jalapeño, seeds removed, roughly chopped

2 tablespoons extra-virgin olive oil

1 teaspoon grated orange zest

¼ cup fresh orange juice (from 1 orange)

1 tablespoon fresh lime juice (from 1 lime)

1 teaspoon honey

¾ teaspoon kosher salt

½ teaspoon ground cumin

½ teaspoon dried oregano

MEATBALLS

1 pound ground pork

2 large eggs

½ cup plain breadcrumbs

Kosher salt

¼ teaspoon freshly cracked black pepper

2 tablespoons vegetable oil

1 to 2 ripe plantains, peeled, cut into ½-inch-thick slices

½ medium red onion, thinly sliced

1 (14-ounce) can black beans, drained and rinsed

Cooked rice, for serving

Serves 6
Prep Time: 15 Minutes
Cook Time: 45 Minutes
Dairy-Free
Gluten-Free
Kid-Friendly

TURKEY MEATBALLS IN RED CURRY SAUCE

You might have noticed that we crush hard on Thai red curry paste. We're loyal to the Mae Ploy brand—not all curry pastes are created equal, and theirs delivers a particularly glorious, vibrant mélange of chilies, coriander, lemongrass, galangal, lime leaves, and shrimp paste. Pairing those warm, fragrant spices with turkey meatballs—not only in the meat mixture, but also in the creamy coconut curry they cook in? Well, yeah. This recipe is kind of next level, even for us.

MEATBALLS

2 pounds ground turkey

⅓ cup finely chopped fresh basil leaves

2 green onions, white and green parts, finely chopped

4 garlic cloves, minced

2 tablespoons fish sauce

1 tablespoon cornstarch

2 tablespoons sugar

2 teaspoons kosher salt

1 teaspoon red curry paste

2 tablespoons vegetable oil

RED CURRY SAUCE

¾ cup finely diced yellow onion

4 garlic cloves, minced

2 tablespoons red curry paste

2 (14-ounce) cans full-fat coconut milk, shaken

3 tablespoons fresh lime juice (from 2 limes)

1 tablespoon fish sauce

1 tablespoon sugar

½ teaspoon fine sea salt

½ cup thinly sliced fresh basil leaves, plus more for garnish

Cooked rice or roasted vegetables, for serving

Fresh cilantro leaves, for garnish (optional)

1. **Make the meatballs.** In a large bowl, combine the turkey, basil, green onions, garlic, fish sauce, cornstarch, sugar, kosher salt, and curry paste. Mix well, then with wet hands, form golf ball–size meatballs (about 2 tablespoons each) and set on a plate. You should have about 20 meatballs.

2. Heat the vegetable oil in a large skillet over medium heat. Once the oil is glistening, working in batches, add the meatballs in a single layer. Cook, undisturbed, until the meatballs are just browned on the bottom, about 3 minutes. Turn them carefully and cook to brown the opposite side, about 3 minutes. Transfer the meatballs back to the plate.

3. **Make the sauce.** Drain off all but 1 tablespoon oil from the skillet and place over medium heat. Add the onion and cook, stirring occasionally, until softened, about 5 minutes. Add the garlic and cook until fragrant, about 1 more minute. Stir in the curry paste. Add the coconut milk and stir vigorously until the paste and milk are fully incorporated and the sauce is smooth. Add the lime juice, fish sauce, sugar, and fine salt. Taste and add more salt as needed.

4. Increase the heat to high and bring to a boil, then return the meatballs to the sauce, discarding any collected juices. Reduce the heat to low, cover, and cook until the sauce has thickened and the meatballs are cooked through, about 20 minutes.

5. Remove the skillet from the heat and stir in the fresh basil. Serve over rice or vegetables, garnished with basil and cilantro, if desired.

MEATBALLS IN BUTTERY MARINARA WITH PESTO GARLIC BREAD

Serves 4 to 6
Prep Time: 20 Minutes
Cook Time: 35 Minutes
Kid-Friendly

A grandma once gave us good advice: If you want to make your company think you've been cooking all day, throw an onion in a skillet right before they arrive. Well, we have a different trick . . . Holly spun up the sauciest kitchen hack ever by combining a jar of marinara sauce with a half stick of butter. Cook hearty, homemade meatballs in the rich, luxurious sauce, then finish it all off with a slice of pesto-slathered cheesy bread. We recommend browning the meatballs to start, but if you're short on time (we've all been there), you can skip that step and just toss them into the sauce. Either way, you'll have a super comforting meal everyone will love—they'll think it simmered on the stove all day.

1. In a large bowl, combine the beef, sausage, breadcrumbs, ½ cup of the Parmesan, the parsley, eggs, garlic, salt, and pepper. Mix well, then with wet hands, form golf ball–size meatballs (about 2 tablespoons each) and place on a plate. You should have about 15 meatballs.

2. Heat the olive oil in a large Dutch oven over medium heat. Once the oil is glistening, working in batches, add the meatballs in a single layer and cook, turning, until well browned all over, about 6 minutes per batch.

3. Return all the browned meatballs to the Dutch oven over medium heat. Add the marinara and 4 tablespoons of the butter to the pan. Cook, stirring, to melt and incorporate the butter, about 2 minutes. Reduce the heat to low, cover, and simmer until the meatballs are cooked through, about 15 minutes.

4. Meanwhile, make the pesto cheese bread. Turn on the broiler.

5. Cut the baguette into 3 equal pieces, then halve each piece crosswise. In a small bowl, use a fork to mash the remaining 4 tablespoons butter together with the pesto. Spread the mixture evenly over each of the bread slices and arrange on a sheet pan. Sprinkle the remaining ½ cup grated Parmesan over the top. Broil for 2 to 3 minutes, until the cheese is browning and bubbly.

6. Divide the meatballs and sauce among bowls. Serve each with a slice of pesto cheese bread alongside.

1 pound 80/20 ground beef

½ pound mild Italian sausage, casings removed

½ cup Italian breadcrumbs

1 cup freshly grated Parmesan cheese

¼ cup finely chopped fresh flat-leaf parsley leaves

2 large eggs, beaten

4 garlic cloves, minced

1½ teaspoons kosher salt

1 teaspoon freshly cracked black pepper

1 tablespoon extra-virgin olive oil

1 (24- to 32-ounce) jar marinara sauce

8 tablespoons (1 stick) salted butter, softened

1 (12-inch) baguette

½ cup Basil Pesto (page 267)

Note: To save even more time, make these—or any—meatballs ahead of time. After you shape them, freeze them on a sheet pan for at least 3 hours, then transfer them to an airtight container and store in the freezer for up to 3 months. When you're ready, drop them right from your freezer into your sauce and simmer for 25 to 30 minutes.

Serves 6

Prep Time: 25 Minutes

Cook Time: 15 Minutes

Dairy-Free

Gluten-Free

Kid-Friendly

MEATBALLS

2 pounds ground pork

1 (5-inch) piece lemongrass, tough outer parts removed, minced (see Note)

1 tablespoon honey

2 teaspoons kosher salt

2 tablespoons minced garlic

4 teaspoons minced peeled fresh ginger

¼ cup packed light brown sugar

¼ cup low-sodium soy sauce or tamari

2 tablespoons rice vinegar

1 teaspoon sriracha

3 teaspoons toasted sesame oil

GREEN ONION OIL

1 bunch green onions, white and green parts, trimmed and thinly sliced

2 tablespoons vegetable oil

1 tablespoon soy sauce or tamari

1 tablespoon rice vinegar

1 tablespoon fish sauce

2 teaspoons minced garlic

2 teaspoons minced peeled fresh ginger

1 pound cooked glass or rice noodles, for serving

Shredded red cabbage, for serving

¼ cup roughly chopped fresh herbs, such as mint, basil, and cilantro, for serving

Note: You should be able to find fresh lemongrass near the fresh ginger at most grocery stores. Look for rigid stalks with tight layers. To prep it, just trim off the root end like you would with a green onion. Peel off any loose outer layers, then slice and dice away!

LEMONGRASS PORK MEATBALLS WITH GLASS NOODLES

If you've never cooked with lemongrass before, we'd like to be the first to welcome you to a whole new world of flavorful, fragrant deliciousness. Lemongrass is a defining ingredient in Vietnamese cuisine, and one of our very favorites—ever. In this recipe, its bright, fresh flavor infuses the pork meatballs, lending the whole dish a lightness and a welcome bite. And best of all? This noodle bowl is equally delicious whether served warm, cold, or even at room temperature, making it incredibly forgiving.

1. Make the meatballs. In a large bowl, combine the ground pork with the lemongrass, honey, salt, 1 tablespoon of the garlic, and 3 teaspoons of the ginger. Mix well, then with wet hands, form golf ball–size meatballs (about 2 tablespoons each) and place on a plate. You should have about 20 meatballs.

2. In a medium bowl, stir together the brown sugar, soy sauce, rice vinegar, the remaining 1 tablespoon garlic, the remaining 1 teaspoon ginger, the sriracha, and ½ teaspoon of the sesame oil.

3. Heat the remaining 2½ teaspoons sesame oil in a large nonstick skillet over medium-high heat. Once the oil is glistening, add the meatballs in a single layer. Cook, undisturbed, until the meatballs are just browned on the bottom, about 3 minutes. Turn them carefully and cook to brown the opposite side, about 3 minutes. Add the soy sauce mixture to the skillet and bring to a boil. Reduce the heat to medium-low to simmer. Cover and cook until the meatballs are cooked through, 5 to 7 minutes.

4. Meanwhile, make the green onion oil. In a small bowl, stir together the green onions, vegetable oil, soy sauce, vinegar, fish sauce, garlic, and ginger to combine.

5. To serve, divide the noodles among 6 bowls. Add red cabbage, then a few meatballs and any sauce left in the pan. Drizzle the green onion oil over the top and sprinkle with fresh herbs.

Serves 6

Prep Time: 15 Minutes

Cook Time: 35 Minutes

Gluten-Free

Kid-Friendly

Vegetarian

CLEAN-OUT-THE-FRIDGE VEGETABLE SOUP

When we were both newly married, we each had our own similar versions of this use-what-you've-got vegetable soup to try to reduce food waste and stretch our budgets as far as possible. More of a template than a recipe, this is an invitation to take liberties. Doctor your soup by adding a Parmesan rind, which will make the broth super savory, or a drizzle of sweet, tart balsamic vinegar to finish. The only must is cooking your aromatics—the onions, carrots, and celery—for at least fifteen minutes at the start. Doing so lays the essential foundation upon which almost any combination of additional flavors can be built. If your pantry could use a clean-out, too, drain a can of beans (white beans are especially good here) and simmer them in during the last five minutes.

2 tablespoons extra-virgin olive oil

1 medium yellow onion, chopped

3 large carrots, peeled and cut into ½-inch-thick rounds

4 celery ribs, cut into 1-inch-thick pieces

3 garlic cloves, minced

1 teaspoon kosher salt

1 teaspoon dried thyme

1 teaspoon dried basil

1 quart vegetable or chicken stock

3 to 4 cups prepared vegetables (see Note)

Parmesan rind or 1 ounce freshly grated Parmesan cheese, plus more grated cheese for serving

Freshly cracked black pepper

Balsamic vinegar, for serving (optional)

1. Heat the olive oil in a large stockpot over medium heat. Once the oil is glistening, add the onion, carrots, and celery and cook, stirring often, until the carrots are softened, 15 to 20 minutes. Add the garlic, salt, thyme, and basil and cook until the garlic is fragrant, about 2 more minutes.

2. Add the stock, vegetables, and Parmesan rind. If your soup needs a bit more liquid, add a cup or two of water. Increase the heat to high and bring to a boil, then reduce the heat to a simmer and cook until the veggies are tender, 5 to 10 minutes. Season to taste with salt and pepper.

3. Ladle the soup into bowls. Garnish with grated Parmesan. Drizzle balsamic vinegar over the top, if desired.

Note: If you need some inspiration, these are some of our favorite veggies to toss in:

- Diced zucchini
- Green beans, roughly chopped
- Corn kernels
- Peas
- Diced potatoes
- Shredded cabbage
- Sliced mushrooms
- Diced bell pepper

WHITE BEAN SOUP WITH HAM AND CHARD

Serves 8
Prep Time: 15 Minutes
Cook Time: 25 Minutes

When Natalie was a kid, visits from her grandmother were defined by food. Grandma Blanche would get off the plane, grocery list in hand, and demand that whichever teenager was old enough to drive take her shopping immediately. Never knowing who'd be coming over, she always planned for a crowd—there were no complaints about that, and rarely any leftovers. Certain recipes bring out these memories more than others, and whenever we have some lingering ham at the holidays, thoughts of Grandma Blanche's white bean soup come rushing back. With plenty of butter and cream, this is an unapologetically stick-to-your-ribs soup, just like grandma's cooking should be. It's sure to feed and please the masses, and maybe make some memories along the way.

1. Heat the butter and olive oil together in a medium pot over medium heat. Once the butter is melted and the oil is glistening, add the leeks and garlic and cook, stirring occasionally, until the leeks are softened, about 4 minutes.

2. Sprinkle the flour over the mixture and stir until incorporated, about 1 minute. Add the beans, stock, milk, cream, thyme, salt, and pepper. Stir to incorporate. Increase the heat to high and bring to a boil, then reduce the heat to a simmer. Cook until the beans are almost falling apart, about 10 minutes.

3. Transfer half the soup to a large bowl. Using an immersion blender, blend the soup in the pot until mostly smooth. (Alternatively, transfer half the soup to the base of a blender, let cool briefly, and blend.) Return the soup to the pot. Stir in the ham and chard. Cook until the ham is warmed through and the greens are wilted, about 3 minutes.

4. Ladle the soup into bowls and top with freshly cracked black pepper. Serve warm, with crusty bread alongside.

2 tablespoons unsalted butter

2 tablespoons extra-virgin olive oil

2 large leeks, trimmed and thinly sliced (see Note on page 199)

3 garlic cloves, minced

¼ cup all-purpose flour

3 (15-ounce) cans white beans, drained and rinsed

1 quart chicken stock

1 cup whole milk

1 cup heavy cream

1 teaspoon fresh thyme leaves

1 teaspoon kosher salt

½ teaspoon freshly cracked black pepper, plus more for serving

2 cups diced cooked ham, cut into bite-size pieces

3 cups stemmed and roughly chopped Swiss chard leaves

Crusty bread, for serving

Serves 6

Prep Time: 10 Minutes

Cook Time: 25 Minutes

<35 Minutes

Dairy-Free

TURMERIC CHICKEN NOODLE SOUP

If there's even a hint of the sniffles in our homes, we get right into the kitchen and make a big batch of this soup. Maybe we're driven by nostalgia—moms always prescribe chicken soup for colds—or maybe we have real faith in the old wives' tale that promises healing in a bowl of chicken soup. The addition of turmeric and ginger, which have anti-inflammatory properties, makes us feel like this golden soup might be even more powerful than our moms'. And whether or not it actually helps to conquer colds, it's without a doubt a one-way ticket to feeling soothed and comforted. And that kind of healing matters, too.

2 tablespoons extra-virgin olive oil

4 green onions, white and green parts, finely chopped (about ½ cup)

½ bunch fresh cilantro, stems minced, leaves reserved for serving

1 tablespoon minced peeled fresh ginger

3 garlic cloves, minced

1 tablespoon ground turmeric

2 quarts chicken stock

3 medium carrots, peeled and cut into ¼-inch-thick slices (1½ cups)

½ teaspoon fine sea salt

¼ teaspoon freshly cracked black pepper

2 (3-ounce) packages ramen noodles, seasoning packets discarded

3 cups shredded chicken (see Note on page 259)

3 cups loosely packed baby spinach

Sriracha or sambal oelek, for serving (optional)

1. Heat the olive oil in a medium stockpot over medium heat. Once the oil is glistening, add the green onions, cilantro stems, and ginger and cook, stirring occasionally, until the onions are softened, about 3 minutes. Stir in the garlic and turmeric and cook until fragrant, about 1 more minute.

2. Add the chicken stock, carrots, salt, and pepper and cook, stirring occasionally, until the carrots are just tender, about 10 minutes. Stir in the noodles, then the chicken and spinach. Increase the heat to high and bring to a boil, then reduce the heat to a simmer and cook until the noodles are tender and the spinach is wilted, about 3 minutes.

3. Ladle the soup into bowls. Top with cilantro leaves and sriracha, if desired, and serve.

SMOKY SAUSAGE AND POTATO STEW

Serves 4
Prep Time: 20 Minutes
Cook Time: 30 Minutes
Dairy-Free
Gluten-Free
Kid-Friendly

Rib-sticking and hearty, this stew takes on a satisfying thickness as it cooks—for only thirty minutes, thanks to starchy potatoes and a good simmer. Smoky, salty, and comforting to the max, this recipe is perfect for a chilly winter day, but we've gladly gobbled it up in the summertime around a roaring campfire, too. If you happen to have any left over, it will taste even better the next day (which we're convinced is the case with just about any stew), making it a great one to make ahead or take to a friend. While we love its thickness, if you're looking for something brothier, just add a bit more stock to thin it out.

1. Heat the olive oil in a medium pot over medium heat. Once the oil is glistening, add the sausage and cook, stirring, until it begins to crisp, about 5 minutes. Transfer to a plate.

2. To the same pot over medium heat, add the onion, bell pepper, and garlic and cook, stirring, until the onion and bell pepper are just tender, about 3 minutes. Add the potatoes and continue to cook until the potatoes are beginning to soften, about another 3 minutes.

3. Pour in the chicken stock. Stir in the crispy sausage and the parsley, paprika, salt, and pepper. Simmer, stirring occasionally, until the potatoes are tender and the flavors are melded, about 20 minutes.

4. Serve the soup in bowls topped with more fresh parsley and with crusty bread alongside, if desired.

2 tablespoons extra-virgin olive oil

12 ounces cooked smoked sausage, cut into ¼-inch-thick slices

1 small yellow onion, diced

1 large red bell pepper, diced

4 garlic cloves, minced

1 pound baby Yukon gold potatoes, cut into ¼-inch-thick slices

3 cups chicken stock

½ cup finely chopped fresh flat-leaf parsley leaves, plus more for serving

1 tablespoon paprika

½ teaspoon fine sea salt

½ teaspoon freshly cracked black pepper

Crusty bread, for serving (optional)

Serves 6

Prep Time: 15 Minutes

Cook Time: 35 Minutes

Gluten-Free

Kid-Friendly

Vegetarian

MINESTRONE WITH BASIL PESTO

While you may have a fixed idea of what minestrone should be, in Italy—where this style originated—*minestrone* refers generally to any kind of thick, rich vegetable soup. Beyond that, you'll find plenty of variation from region to region and season to season. Our version takes a cue from minestrone you'd find in Liguria, the home of fresh basil pesto. Along that sun-soaked riviera, minestrone is traditionally finished with a spoonful of the stuff, and we think you'll agree it's a pretty genius move. While you can certainly buy it, we love to make our own—it's super quick and easy.

2 tablespoons extra-virgin olive oil

1 small yellow onion, diced

2 celery ribs, diced

2 large carrots, peeled and diced

5 garlic cloves, minced

1 quart vegetable or chicken stock

1 (15-ounce) can tomato sauce

1 (15-ounce) can diced tomatoes

6 ounces green beans, trimmed and cut into 2-inch pieces (about 1 cup)

1 tablespoon Italian seasoning

1½ teaspoons kosher salt

½ teaspoon freshly cracked black pepper

1 (15.5-ounce) can kidney beans, drained and rinsed

1 cup ditalini or other short-cut pasta

Basil Pesto (page 267), for serving

1. Heat the olive oil in a large pot over medium heat. Once the oil is glistening, add the onion, celery, and carrots. Cook, stirring occasionally, until softened, about 7 minutes. Add the garlic and cook until fragrant, about 1 more minute.

2. Add the stock, tomato sauce, diced tomatoes and their juices, green beans, Italian seasoning, salt, and pepper. Increase the heat to high and bring to a boil, then reduce the heat to a simmer. Cook until the green beans are beginning to soften, about 10 minutes. Add the kidney beans and pasta. Cook, stirring often, until the pasta is al dente, about 10 more minutes.

3. Ladle the soup into bowls. Top with a spoonful of pesto before serving.

Serves 6
Prep Time: 10 Minutes
Cook Time: 35 Minutes
Dairy-Free
Gluten-Free
Kid-Friendly

LEMON CHICKEN AND RICE SOUP WITH GREEN BEANS

Somewhere between Greek avgolemono soup and traditional American chicken soup, this herby, lemon-laced pot of sunshine is anything but boring. It's the kind of soup you hope your kids come home for, the kind of soup you wish a friend would drop off on your doorstep when you've had a bad day. And, in case we haven't said it loud enough yet, this recipe is yet another chance for a store-bought rotisserie chicken to save the day and make your life (and dinner) oh so easy.

2 tablespoons extra-virgin olive oil

½ small yellow onion, diced

2 garlic cloves, minced

¾ cup short-grain rice, rinsed

¾ pound green beans, trimmed and cut into 2-inch pieces (2 cups)

⅓ cup fresh lemon juice (from about 3 lemons)

2 tablespoons chopped fresh dill, plus more for garnish

½ teaspoon dried oregano

1½ teaspoons kosher salt, plus more to taste

½ teaspoon freshly cracked black pepper, plus more to taste

1 quart chicken stock

2 cups shredded chicken (see Note on page 259)

Note: If you prefer a thinner soup, simply add more liquid. Of course, stock is most flavorful, but you can always add more water, too. This method applies to virtually any soup.

1. Heat the olive oil in a large pot over medium heat. Once the oil is glistening, add the onion and cook, stirring occasionally, until softened and translucent, about 5 minutes. Add the garlic and rice and cook, stirring often, until the rice is opaque, about 2 minutes.

2. Pour in 1½ cups water. Increase the heat to high and bring to a boil, then reduce the heat to a simmer. Cover and cook until the rice is almost tender and most of the water has been absorbed, about 10 minutes.

3. Add the green beans, lemon juice, dill, oregano, salt, and pepper. Pour in the chicken stock and 1 cup water. Increase the heat to high and bring to a boil, then reduce the heat to a simmer. Cook, uncovered, until the green beans are just tender, about 8 minutes. Stir in the chicken to warm through, about 3 more minutes. Season to taste with more salt and pepper.

4. Ladle the soup into bowls and serve topped with more dill.

CHICKEN AND BARLEY
SOUP

Serves 6
Prep Time: 20 Minutes
Cook Time: 35 Minutes
Dairy-Free

If you've never cooked with barley before, jump on in! This nutty, chewy ancient grain is good for more than just making beer. We love to use it in soups such as this light, brothy one because it holds its texture so well. Even left over, the barley will maintain some bite rather than turn to mush. It's a health superstar, too, with a lot of fiber, as well as a host of vitamins and a significant amount of protein. To make this soothing bowl even more nutritious, we add a handful of fragrant herbs and plenty of kale. While we call for pepper to taste, we recommend adding it with a very heavy hand!

1. Heat the olive oil in a large stockpot over medium-high heat. Once the oil is glistening, add the onion and celery and cook, stirring occasionally, until the onion is softened, about 5 minutes. Add the garlic and cook until fragrant, about 1 more minute.

2. Add the chicken stock, increase the heat to high, and bring to a boil. Add the barley and salt. Reduce the heat to medium-low, cover, and cook until the barley is tender but still has some bite, 20 to 25 minutes.

3. Add the chicken, kale, parsley, and chives. Continue to cook until the chicken is heated through and the kale is wilted, about 5 minutes.

4. Adjust the salt to taste, then add as much lemon juice and freshly cracked pepper as you like. Garnish the soup with the radishes and more chives before serving.

2 tablespoons extra-virgin olive oil

1 small yellow onion, chopped

2 celery ribs, cut into ½-inch pieces

4 garlic cloves, minced

6 cups chicken stock

½ cup pearl barley

½ teaspoon kosher salt

3 cups shredded chicken (see Note on page 259)

2 cups packed stemmed and roughly torn Tuscan kale

2 tablespoons minced fresh flat-leaf parsley leaves

1 tablespoon chopped fresh chives, plus more for serving

1 lemon

Freshly cracked black pepper

2 to 3 radishes, thinly sliced or cut into matchsticks, for serving

Serves 8
Prep Time: 10 Minutes
Cook Time: 20 Minutes
<35 Minutes
Dairy-Free
Gluten-Free
Kid-Friendly

CARNITAS IN A STEW

If you're as crazy for carnitas as we are, you're always on the hunt for more ways to enjoy the tender, generously seasoned bites of pork. When you've eaten your fill of tacos and burritos, it's time to make this seriously substantial stew. While you'll need a whole batch of carnitas to make it—and yes, that takes a little while—once your carnitas are done, the rest comes together fast. You might even plan ahead and make the carnitas over the weekend. With a batch waiting for you in the fridge, a big, aromatic pot of this exquisite, meaty dish is just about thirty minutes away.

2 tablespoons extra-virgin olive oil

1 small yellow onion, diced

1 teaspoon kosher salt

1 teaspoon garlic powder

1 teaspoon chili powder

1 teaspoon ground cumin

¼ teaspoon freshly cracked black pepper

1 quart chicken stock

1 recipe Carnitas (page 161)

1 (15-ounce can) white beans, drained and rinsed

1 cup Salsa Verde (page 271)

FOR SERVING
Thinly sliced radish

Crumbled Cotija cheese

Chopped fresh cilantro

Pepitas

Sliced avocado

1. Heat the olive oil in a large stockpot over medium-high heat. Once the oil is glistening, add the onion and cook, stirring occasionally, until softened and translucent, about 5 minutes. Add the salt, garlic powder, chili powder, cumin, and pepper and cook, stirring constantly, until fragrant, about 30 seconds.

2. Add the chicken stock, 2 cups water, the carnitas, white beans, and salsa verde. Increase the heat to high and bring to a boil. Then reduce the heat to medium-low and cook until the flavors are melded and everything is warmed through, about 10 minutes.

3. Serve family-style with an array of the toppings of your choice.

CREAMY BROCCOLI SOUP WITH ROASTED GARLIC

Serves 4
Prep Time: 15 Minutes
Cook Time: 40 Minutes
Gluten-Free

If you know us well, you know we do not shy away from garlic. In this soup, we call for two whole heads of the stuff! Trimmed then roasted, it takes on a sweet, mild flavor and almost melty texture. If you don't have the time (or the patience) for that, hit up the olive bar at your local market where you can purchase it premade. You'll need about ⅓ cup for this recipe, but it's not a bad idea to load up and add it to everything you can imagine. Holly first cooked up this soup when she was recovering from a cold and hoping for a little extra power. She's not sure it's all the garlic that actually sped up her recovery, but she still makes this soup any time she feels the sniffles coming on, as it's rich and comforting and always seems to help. And sometimes a little comfort food is all that's needed to cure what ails you.

2 heads garlic

1 tablespoon extra-virgin olive oil

4 ounces pancetta or bacon, diced

1 small yellow onion, chopped

1 quart chicken stock

1 pound broccoli florets (from 2 crowns)

½ teaspoon fine sea salt

½ teaspoon freshly cracked black pepper, plus more for serving

1 cup heavy cream

½ cup freshly grated Parmesan cheese

1. Preheat the oven to 425°F.

2. Trim the tops off the garlic heads just enough to expose the cloves. Place each head on a separate piece of aluminum foil. Pour the olive oil over the exposed cloves. Wrap the foil around each head of garlic and place on a sheet pan. Roast the garlic for about 35 minutes, or until golden brown and soft. Remove from the oven and let cool in the foil.

3. Meanwhile, in a large soup pot over medium heat, cook the pancetta, stirring occasionally, until crispy, 5 to 7 minutes. Using a slotted spoon, transfer the pancetta to a bowl, reserving the rendered fat in the pot.

4. Add the onion to the pot and cook over medium heat, stirring occasionally, until softened and translucent, about 5 minutes. If browned bits are stuck to the bottom, add a splash of the chicken stock and scrape them up with a wooden spoon. Then add the broccoli florets, the remaining stock, the salt, and the pepper to the pot. Increase the heat to high and bring to a boil, then reduce the heat to low and simmer until the broccoli is tender, 3 to 5 minutes. Once the roasted garlic is cool enough to handle, squeeze it out of its skins and into the pot of soup.

5. Use an immersion blender to blend the soup directly in the pot. (Alternatively, transfer the soup to the base of a blender, let cool briefly, and blend until smooth. Then pour the soup back into the pot.) Stir in the cream and cook until warmed through, 2 to 3 minutes.

6. Serve the soup warm, topped with the crispy pancetta, the Parmesan, and freshly cracked pepper.

Serves 4 to 6

Prep Time: 25 Minutes

Cook Time: 30 Minutes

Dairy-Free

Gluten-Free

Kid-Friendly

COCONUT CHICKEN SOUP WITH KABOCHA SQUASH

Harvested in early fall, but usually available all winter long, kabocha squash has quickly become one of our favorite cool-weather ingredients. If you don't see it at your grocery store, try looking at a farmers' market or natural foods store, where you're more likely to score some. Even if you can't track it down, the flavors of this Japanese pumpkin are similar enough to a sweet potato that you can make a simple swap and still get the right result. Don't be tempted to use another squash, though. They aren't quite as sweet as kabocha, and they're a bit more watery.

1 quart chicken stock

1 (14-ounce) can full-fat coconut milk, shaken

1 small sweet onion, halved and thinly sliced

4 garlic cloves, minced

1 tablespoon minced peeled fresh ginger

1 tablespoon light brown sugar

1 tablespoon red curry paste

3 to 4 cups cubed kabocha squash or sweet potato (about 1¾ pounds)

1 pound boneless, skinless chicken breast, thinly sliced crosswise

2 teaspoons fish sauce

1 teaspoon kosher salt

Fresh cilantro, for serving (optional)

Sliced green onions, for serving (optional)

1. In a large stockpot over high heat, combine the chicken stock, coconut milk, onion, garlic, ginger, brown sugar, and curry paste. Bring to a boil. Cook, whisking to fully incorporate the curry paste, until the onion is softened and the flavors are melded, about 8 minutes.

2. Add the squash and return to a boil. Cook until nearly tender, about 10 minutes. Add the chicken and the fish sauce. Reduce the heat to medium-low and cook until the chicken is opaque, firm, and cooked through, about 5 minutes. Add the salt and adjust to taste.

3. Ladle the soup into bowls and top with cilantro and green onions, if desired.

CREAMY TORTELLINI SOUP WITH SAUSAGE AND KALE

Serves 6
Prep Time: 15 Minutes
Cook Time: 30 Minutes
Kid-Friendly

If we could be so bold as to claim that one of our recipes has become *iconic*—at least in the Internet food world—this soup is it. After we shared the recipe on our blog, we had our first encounter with viral popularity. Watching people make it again and again was a highlight that fall, but watching people continue to make it with the same excitement years later is even better. Honestly, we get why people love this soup. Rooted in a garlicky tomato bisque, it's brimming with the really good stuff: cheesy tortellini, sausage, and kale. Best of all? It comes together in less than an hour.

1. Heat the olive oil in a large pot over medium-high heat. Once the oil is glistening, add the sausage, onion, and garlic and cook, breaking up the sausage with a wooden spoon, until it is browned and the onion is translucent, about 5 minutes. Add the tomato paste, stirring to combine, about 1 minute.

2. Add the chicken stock and crushed tomatoes. Bring to a boil and add the salt, then reduce the heat to a simmer and cook until slightly reduced, about 15 minutes. Stir in the kale, tortellini, and cream. Cook until the kale is wilted and the pasta is tender, 3 to 5 minutes. Adjust the seasoning to taste.

3. Ladle the soup into bowls. Top with red pepper flakes and Parmesan, if desired, before serving.

1 tablespoon extra-virgin olive oil

1 pound mild Italian sausage, casings removed

1 small yellow onion, finely diced

6 garlic cloves, minced

2 tablespoons tomato paste

1 quart chicken stock

1 (14.5-ounce can) crushed tomatoes

1 teaspoon kosher salt

4 cups packed stemmed and roughly torn curly kale

10 ounces fresh cheese tortellini (see Note)

1 cup heavy cream

¼ teaspoon red pepper flakes, for serving (optional)

Freshly shaved or grated Parmesan cheese, for serving (optional)

Note: Fresh tortellini—and other fresh pastas—will be found in the refrigerated section of your grocery store, separate from the dried pastas.

Serves 6
Prep Time: 20 Minutes
Cook Time: 40 Minutes
Dairy-Free
Gluten-Free
Vegetarian

CURRY LENTIL SOUP

Black lentils, also called beluga lentils, are small, caviar-like, and ideal for a soup like this one because they really hold their shape, even after a long simmer. We cook them separately before adding them to the soup because they have a tendency to dye their cooking liquid a dark shade of gray, and we don't want anything to muddy this soup's creamy, bright yellow curry broth. Speaking of curry, be sure your curry powder is fresh—purchased within the last six months—and high-quality, because it is the defining flavor of the soup. It's make or break! Otherwise, this recipe is easy breezy. Oh, and if you use veggie stock instead of chicken, it's vegan, too.

1¾ teaspoons fine sea salt

1 cup black lentils

2 tablespoons extra-virgin olive oil

1 small yellow onion, chopped

1 tablespoon grated peeled fresh ginger

4 garlic cloves, minced

3 tablespoons yellow curry powder

½ teaspoon ground cinnamon

4 cups vegetable or chicken stock

2 (13.5-ounce) cans full-fat coconut milk, shaken

3 medium carrots, peeled and cut into ½-inch-thick rounds (about 3 cups)

4 cups packed stemmed and roughly torn curly kale

1. Fill a medium pot with 6 cups water and add 1 teaspoon of the salt. Bring to a boil over high heat. Add the lentils, give them a stir, and cook until nearly tender, about 35 minutes. Drain.

2. Meanwhile, heat the olive oil in a large stockpot over medium heat. Once the oil is glistening, add the onion and cook, stirring occasionally, until softened and translucent, about 5 minutes. Add the ginger and garlic and cook until fragrant, another 1 to 2 minutes. Stir in the curry powder and cinnamon.

3. Pour in the stock and coconut milk and stir to combine. Add the carrots, increase the heat to high, and bring the soup to a boil. Reduce the heat to a simmer and cook until the carrots are tender, 6 to 8 minutes. Stir in the lentils. Add the kale and the remaining ¾ teaspoon salt and cook until the kale is wilted, 3 to 5 minutes.

4. Ladle the soup into bowls and serve warm.

TORTILLA SOUP

Serves 6
Prep Time: 20 Minutes
Cook Time: 40 Minutes
Dairy-Free
Gluten-Free
Kid-Friendly

This quick dump-and-simmer version of a popular soup came about as Holly's solution to a meal that was easy enough for a busy Wednesday, but impressive enough to serve for company. It achieved its goal that night, and it was so good that we've kept making it. Simple to make yet smoky and layered, this soup has even been called "restaurant quality" by those who've had it. Plus, with lots of topping choices, everyone can customize their own. While nothing in here is fancy, the sum of the parts is a really wonderful dish that we make on repeat for any occasion.

1. In a large soup pot, combine the shredded chicken, chicken stock, creamed corn, the tomatoes and their juices, the enchilada sauce, onion, zucchini, chilies, garlic, bay leaves, cumin, chili powder, salt, and pepper. Place the pot over high heat and bring the soup to a boil, then reduce the heat to medium-low and cook, stirring occasionally, until the onion is softened and translucent and the zucchini is tender, about 30 minutes. Season to taste and discard the bay leaves.

2. Serve the soup in bowls topped with tortilla strips, and any additional toppings of your choice, as desired.

1 roasted chicken, shredded (3 to 4 cups) (see Note)

1 quart chicken stock

1 (14.75-ounce) can creamed corn

1 (14.5-ounce) can diced fire-roasted tomatoes

1 (10-ounce) can red enchilada sauce

1 small yellow onion, chopped

1 medium zucchini, chopped

1 (4-ounce) can green chilies

4 large garlic cloves, minced

3 bay leaves

1 teaspoon ground cumin

1 teaspoon chili powder

1 teaspoon kosher salt

¼ teaspoon freshly cracked black pepper

Tortilla strips

FOR SERVING (OPTIONAL)
Chopped fresh cilantro
Fresh lime juice
Sour cream
Shredded cheddar or pepper Jack cheese
Diced avocado

Note: Chicken is easier to pull off the bones and shred when it's warm. We like to purchase rotisserie chicken from the store and pick off all the meat before storing it in the refrigerator—that way it's ready to go whenever we want to use it.

259

Serves 6

Prep Time: 15 Minutes

Cook Time: 45 Minutes

Gluten-Free

SPICY SALMON CHOWDER

Maybe you think seafood chowder is hard to make. And maybe you're right! If we're talking about clam chowder, at least, most recipes are quite fussy. You have to steam a bunch of clams, then deal with all of those shells. Count us out. But salmon chowder, on the other hand, is way easier to make, and every bit as briny and creamy as its clammy cousin. We've taken the liberty of adding jalapeños to the mix for a spicy lift that counters this chowder's buttery richness. If the heat is not for you, try discarding the jalapeño seeds—that's where all the spiciness lives.

4 tablespoons (½ stick) unsalted butter

8 ounces bacon, cut into ½-inch pieces

1 bunch green onions, white and green parts, finely chopped

3 celery ribs, minced

1 small yellow onion, minced

1 jalapeño, thinly sliced, plus more for garnish

4 garlic cloves, minced

1 quart seafood or chicken stock

2 large russet potatoes, peeled and cut into 1½-inch pieces

1½ teaspoons fine sea salt

½ teaspoon freshly cracked black pepper, plus more for serving

1 tablespoon cornstarch

2 cups frozen corn

2 cups heavy cream

1½ pounds salmon, preferably wild, skin discarded and cut into 1½-inch pieces

1. In a large, heavy stockpot, melt the butter over medium heat. Add the bacon and cook, stirring often, until the bacon begins to crisp, about 8 minutes. Using a slotted spoon, remove the bacon from the pan and set aside.

2. Reserve ¼ cup green onions. Add the remaining green onions, the celery, onion, jalapeño, and garlic and cook over medium heat, stirring often, until the onion is softened, about 5 minutes. Add the stock, potatoes, crisped bacon, 1 teaspoon of the salt, and the pepper. Simmer, stirring occasionally, until the potatoes are tender, about 15 minutes.

3. In a small bowl, whisk together the cornstarch and 2 tablespoons water to form a slurry. Stir the slurry into the broth and bring to a boil over high heat. Cook until slightly thickened, about 2 minutes. Reduce the heat to a gentle simmer and stir in the corn and cream, then return the chowder to a simmer. Add the salmon and season it with the remaining ½ teaspoon salt. Cover and simmer until the salmon is cooked through, about 10 minutes. Taste and adjust the salt as needed.

4. To serve, ladle the chowder into bowls. Top with the reserved green onions and additional black pepper. Add more jalapeños for extra heat.

THINGS FOR DIPPING, SPREADING, AND DRESSING

Makes ½ cup
Prep Time: 5 Minutes

BBQ SPICE RUB

A little bit smoky and a little bit sweet, this homemade spice rub goes well with just about anything you'd want to throw on your grill. Even if you're not grilling, it will lend deep, fiery notes in just the same way.

2 tablespoons dark brown sugar

1½ tablespoons kosher salt

1 tablespoon paprika

1 tablespoon chili powder

1 tablespoon onion powder

1 tablespoon garlic powder

2 teaspoons freshly cracked black pepper

In a small bowl, stir together the sugar, salt, paprika, chili powder, onion powder, garlic powder, and pepper. Store in an airtight container at room temperature for up to 1 year.

Makes ½ cup
Prep Time: 5 Minutes

EVERYTHING BAGEL SEASONING

The everything bagel is queen of all the bagels. And this seasoning blend is good on . . . everything. Try sprinkling it over plain rice, scrambled eggs, toast, sliced avocado, your favorite salad, and, yup, everything in between.

2 tablespoons dried minced garlic

2 tablespoons dried minced onion

1½ tablespoons sesame seeds (black, white, or a combination)

½ tablespoon poppy seeds

2 teaspoons kosher salt

In a small bowl, stir together the garlic, onion, sesame seeds, poppy seeds, and salt. Store at room temperature in an airtight container for up to 1 year.

CARAMELIZED ONIONS

Makes 1¾ cups
Prep Time: 10 Minutes
Cook Time: 60 Minutes

Cooking low and slow is key here. It pulls out the natural sweetness in the onions, making them jammy and delicious. If you'd like yours even sweeter, you can stir in a bit of brown sugar at the end of cooking.

1. In a large nonstick skillet, heat the butter and olive oil together over medium heat. Once the butter is melted, add the onions and cook, stirring often, until softened and translucent, about 10 minutes. Reduce the heat to medium-low, spread the onions into a single layer, and cook, stirring every 10 to 15 minutes, then returning the onions to a single layer, until the onions are golden brown and caramelized, 45 to 60 minutes total. If the onions are browning too quickly, add water, 1 tablespoon at a time, until they stop browning and return to caramelizing.

2. Taste and add salt as needed. Stir in the brown sugar, if desired. Store refrigerated in an airtight container for up to 1 week.

2 tablespoons unsalted butter

2 tablespoons extra-virgin olive oil

1½ pounds yellow onions (about 3 large), halved and cut into ¼-inch-thick slices

Fine sea salt

1 teaspoon light brown sugar (optional)

TACO SEASONING

Making your own taco seasoning not only means steering clear of the preservatives and sodium overload in store-bought spice packets, but also means you can adjust the spice ratios to suit your own tastes.

In a small bowl, stir together the chili powder, paprika, cumin, onion powder, garlic powder, oregano, salt, and pepper. Store at room temperature in an airtight container for up to 1 year.

1 tablespoon chili powder

1 tablespoon smoked paprika

1 tablespoon ground cumin

1 tablespoon onion powder

1 tablespoon garlic powder

1 tablespoon dried oregano

1 tablespoon fine sea salt

½ tablespoon freshly cracked black pepper

BASIL PESTO

Makes 1½ cups
Prep Time: 10 Minutes

Be mindful not to overdo it when you blend this pesto, as you want to keep the texture a bit coarse. It calls to mind the traditional mortar and pestle, but you still get the convenience of a food processor.

In the base of a food processor, combine the basil, cheese, pine nuts, garlic, and salt. Pulse 20 times until just blended. With the processor running on low, slowly pour in the olive oil. Store refrigerated in an airtight container for up to 1 week, or in the freezer for up to 3 months.

2 cups packed fresh basil leaves (about 2½ ounces)

1 cup freshly grated Parmesan cheese

¼ cup pine nuts

2 garlic cloves

½ teaspoon fine sea salt

1 cup extra-virgin olive oil

Note: We love to portion this pesto into an ice cube tray and freeze it so we always have it ready to go.

Makes 2 cups
Prep Time: 5 Minutes

PICKLED ONIONS

Quickly pickled in a bath of seasoned vinegar, these tart, magenta half-moons add a punch of flavor to anything they touch. Use them in salads or on sandwiches, tacos, or burgers . . . trust us, you'll always be happy you have them on hand.

2 cups distilled white vinegar

4 whole cloves

1 garlic clove, halved

2 teaspoons sugar

2 teaspoons kosher salt

1 bay leaf

1 cinnamon stick

1 large red onion, halved and thinly sliced

4 cups boiling water

1. In a 1-quart glass jar, stir together the vinegar, cloves, garlic, sugar, salt, bay leaf, and cinnamon stick until the sugar dissolves.

2. Place the onion slices in a mesh strainer set over the sink. Slowly pour the boiling water over the onions. Using tongs, immediately transfer the hot onions to the vinegar mixture. Gently press the onions down to fully submerge.

3. Seal the jar and let the onions pickle, refrigerated, for at least 1 hour before using, preferably overnight. Store refrigerated for up to 3 weeks.

SALSA VERDE

Makes 3 cups
Prep Time: 5 Minutes
Cook Time: 25 Minutes, plus cooling time

Salsa verde, or green salsa, is good just about anywhere you want to add a bit of heat. Depending how spicy you like yours, you might want to add the jalapeños incrementally—or even remove their seeds for a milder version. Taste as you go, and stop when the fire hits the right note.

2 tablespoons vegetable oil

10 to 12 medium tomatillos, husked (about 1½ pounds)

1 large white onion, quartered

1 to 3 jalapeños, stems removed, seeded if desired

4 garlic cloves

1 bunch fresh cilantro, stems removed

1 teaspoon fine sea salt

1. Heat the vegetable oil in a large pot over high heat. Once the oil is glistening, add the tomatillos, 2 of the onion quarters, the jalapeños, and the garlic in a single layer. Cook, undisturbed, until the ingredients are charred on the bottom, about 5 minutes. Flip and repeat on the other side, about 5 more minutes. Reduce the heat to low, cover, and cook for 15 minutes, or until charred. Remove the pot from the heat, uncover, and let cool completely, about 30 minutes.

2. Transfer the charred ingredients to the base of a blender or food processor. Add the remaining 2 onion quarters, the cilantro, and salt. Pulse until your desired texture is achieved.

3. Store refrigerated in an airtight container for up to 1 week.

CHIMICHURRI

Makes 1⅓ cups
Prep Time: 5 Minutes

Chimichurri is most closely associated with Argentinian cuisine, where it's often used to dress up simple grilled steak. Unsurprisingly, though, we think it's good on just about anything.

1 small shallot, cut into wedges

¾ cup fresh flat-leaf parsley leaves

2 garlic cloves

1 tablespoon fresh oregano leaves

1½ teaspoons kosher salt

1 teaspoon freshly cracked black pepper

¾ cup extra-virgin olive oil

¼ cup red wine vinegar

½ teaspoon red pepper flakes

In the base of a food processor, combine the shallot, parsley, garlic, oregano, salt, and pepper. Pulse until well combined, but still slightly chunky. Transfer the mixture to a small bowl. Add the oil, vinegar, and red pepper flakes. Stir to combine. Store refrigerated in an airtight container for up to 2 weeks.

Makes 1¼ cups
Prep Time: 5 Minutes

HONEY MUSTARD VINAIGRETTE

In addition to the obvious honey and mustard, shallot and rice vinegar bring bright acidity, sweetness, and mild heat to this dressing, while a good pour of olive oil makes it creamy. Mixing in a blender instead of by hand means speedy and stress-free emulsification. You'll want to pour this on everything!

½ cup extra-virgin olive oil

⅓ cup rice vinegar

½ small shallot, roughly chopped

2 tablespoons stone-ground mustard

2 tablespoons honey

½ teaspoon fine sea salt

¼ teaspoon freshly cracked black pepper

In the base of a blender or food processor, combine the oil, vinegar, shallot, mustard, honey, salt, and pepper. Blend until creamy and smooth, 2 to 4 minutes. Store refrigerated in an airtight container for up to 1 week.

Makes 1½ cups
Prep Time: 5 Minutes

GREEN GODDESS DRESSING

These days, everyone seems to have a slightly different take on this dressing, but it's always green, mayo-based, and wonderfully tangy thanks to plenty of garlic and lemon. Many people add anchovies, but we've opted to keep ours fish-free and instead let the herbs do the talking.

¾ cup mayonnaise

⅓ cup packed fresh cilantro leaves

4 green onions, ends trimmed, roughly chopped

4 to 6 garlic cloves

10 large fresh basil leaves

2 tablespoons fresh lemon juice (from 1 lemon)

½ teaspoon fine sea salt

In the base of a blender or food processor, combine the mayonnaise, cilantro, green onions, garlic, basil, lemon juice, and salt. Blend until smooth, 2 to 4 minutes. Store refrigerated in an airtight container for up to 1 week.

Makes 1½ cups
Prep Time: 5 Minutes

BUTTERMILK RANCH DRESSING

Fighting words, we know, but we really think this is the best ranch dressing recipe, ever. Use fresh parsley if you've got it, but dried works fine, too.

½ cup buttermilk

½ cup mayonnaise

½ cup sour cream

2 teaspoons minced fresh flat-leaf parsley leaves or 1 teaspoon dried parsley

1 teaspoon onion powder

1 teaspoon garlic powder

1 teaspoon dried dill

½ teaspoon fine sea salt

In a small bowl, whisk together the buttermilk, mayonnaise, sour cream, parsley, onion powder, garlic powder, dill, and salt until smooth. Store refrigerated in an airtight container for up to 2 weeks.

ROMESCO SAUCE

Makes 3½ cups
Prep Time: 5 Minutes

Be sure to use fire-roasted tomatoes and roasted red peppers here—no substitutions, please! That smoky wood-fire flavor is the key to balancing this tangy Catalonian sauce. When blending, you're looking for a texture somewhere right in the middle of chunky and just smooth, like the consistency of pesto.

In the base of a blender or food processor, combine the tomatoes, red peppers, almonds, pine nuts, parsley, oil, garlic, vinegar, paprika, and salt. Blend until your desired consistency is reached, about 1 minute. Store refrigerated in an airtight container for up to 2 weeks.

1 (14-ounce) can fire-roasted tomatoes, drained

1 (12-ounce) jar roasted red peppers, drained

¾ cup blanched almonds

¼ cup pine nuts (see Note)

¼ cup fresh flat-leaf parsley leaves

¼ cup extra-virgin olive oil

3 garlic cloves, smashed

2 tablespoons sherry vinegar

1 teaspoon smoked paprika

1 teaspoon fine sea salt

Note: If you don't have pine nuts handy, you can use hazelnuts or more almonds.

PEANUT SAUCE

Makes about 2½ cups
Prep Time: 5 Minutes
Cook Time: 15 Minutes

After a lot of trial and error, we've landed on a peanut sauce that's as close to perfection as we've ever come. It keeps in the fridge for up to a week. If it separates, just give it a little whisk over low heat to reincorporate everything.

1. In a small saucepan over medium-low heat, combine the coconut milk, peanut butter, ⅓ cup water, the brown sugar, vinegar, sambal oelek, and salt. Bring to a simmer and cook, stirring constantly, until the ingredients are well combined, about 5 minutes.

2. Remove the pan from the heat and let the sauce thicken for at least 10 minutes. Transfer to an airtight container and store refrigerated for up to 1 week.

1⅓ cups full-fat coconut milk (shaken in can before measuring)

½ cup unsweetened creamy peanut butter

¼ cup light brown sugar

2 tablespoons rice vinegar

1 tablespoon sambal oelek or other chili paste

1 teaspoon fine sea salt

Makes about ½ cup
Prep Time: 10 Minutes

HERB BUTTER

This recipe could really be called *Any* Herb Butter because the technique works well with just about any fresh herb you love, adding bright flavor wherever it goes. It's a great way to preserve the bounty of your garden, too.

½ cup (1 stick) unsalted butter, softened

3 tablespoons minced fresh herbs

1½ teaspoons fine sea salt

1. In a small bowl, combine the butter, herbs, and salt. Mix well to incorporate evenly and completely.

2. Transfer the butter to a piece of parchment. Using the paper, roll the butter into a log about 4 inches long and 1½ inches wide. Close the parchment paper around it and twist the ends to seal. Refrigerate the butter until firm, about 1 hour.

3. Wrap the butter and parchment in plastic wrap or place in an airtight container. Store in the refrigerator for up to 1 week or in the freezer for up to 3 months. Unwrap and slice to use.

Acknowledgments

To our husbands, Mort and Scott, you're the hardest working dads we know. Thank you for creating a way for us to pursue our dreams and for being our biggest cheerleaders. We'll never forget the dishes you washed, the school days you managed, and the meals you cooked in the middle of a global pandemic just so we could give this book everything we had. You're our favorites. xoxox

To our agent, Andrea Barzvi, we cry when we think of you. We're not sure we would have ever had the guts to attempt writing this book if it wasn't for you believing in us. Thank you for answering every call, text, and email. You truly are a saint—a really smart saint.

To our photographer, Eva Kolenko, we knew the moment we saw your work that you were the one we wanted for this book. You brought life to every recipe in a way that we had only dreamed of. Thank you for all the laughs, feedback, and encouragement. We're so damn lucky to have your photographs in our book.

To our readers, especially those who have been with us from the beginning and have been patiently and subtly begging us to write a cookbook for many years, whether you are raising your kids on TMP recipes, winning over a first date, or just trying to eat a good meal after a long day at work, we're so happy to know you trust us. You're the real reason we took this on.

To our friends Fairlight and Katie, who rolled up their sleeves and helped us test sixty-five recipes in five days, you washed so many dishes and cut so many onions. Seriously, thank you for making those long days fun.

To all our other friends and family who ate the food we cooked and gave encouraging feedback over and over, thank you for not letting a single bite go to waste. To all the friends who gave advice and input on design when we were indecisive, you're our heroes. To all the friends who just listened to us as we worked on this book, your ears never seemed to grow tired. We adore you!

To Danielle and Case, thank you for testing every single one of these recipes, sometimes more than once. Your impeccable taste buds and attention to detail are on every page of this book.

To Emily Caneer, for every steak you browned, every cheese top you broiled, and every herb you meticulously placed, thanks a million times over. Your attention to detail in perfecting a dish is the invitation we hoped to share with each recipe!

To Claire Mack, thank you for your great taste and for providing your perfectly curated collection of plates, glasses, cutlery, and the like. Can we live in your studio when we grow up?

To our book designer, Laura Palese, thank you for designing this book with all of our ideas in mind. It's perfect, and we are forever grateful for your attention to all the little things!

To our editor, Justin Schwartz, thank you for believing in us from day one! Your editorial eye carried us to the finish line with incredible wisdom and guidance.

To Miranda Rake, you brought a voice to our brand that we weren't capable of finding on our own. You've challenged the way we look at food and the way in which we share recipes. From the bottom of our hearts, thank you for taking our stories and putting them into beautiful words.

To Amanda Englander, your editing, writing, organization, and overall management made it possible to deliver this book on time. Thank you for all the laughs, even on the boring stuff. Your voice and em-dashes are all over this book. We couldn't have pulled it off without you.

To Luke and Mallory, thank you for capturing our families (including Bruce the dog) so beautifully (including Bruce the dog) in all their chaotic glory!

To Holly, thank you for making every late-night call about more than just the book. I can't imagine having done this with another soul, and I'm so proud of what we've accomplished. —Natalie

To Natalie, the best "work wife" a gal could ask for. Love that we get to share all of our work wins and accomplishments with each other. There's no one else I'd rather celebrate this book with. —Holly

Index